The City
After the Automobile

ALSO BY MOSHE SAFDIE

Beyond Habitat

For Everyone a Garden

Form and Purpose

The Harvard-Jerusalem Studio:
Urban Designs for the Holy City

Beyond Habitat by 20 Years

The Language and Medium of Architecture

Jerusalem: The Future of the Past

The City
After the Automobile

An Architect's Vision

MOSHE SAFDIE
with Wendy Kohn

Westview Press
A Member of the Perseus Books Group

Text and illustrations copyright © 1997 by Moshe Safdie

Harvey Wiley Corbett (1873–1954), *La ville future. Une solution hardie du problème de la circulation.* (The City of the Future. An innovative solution to the traffic problem.) Reprinted from *Scientific American,* supplied by Collection Centre Canadien d'Architecture/Canadian Centre for Architecture, Montréal.

Le Corbusier, "Cité contemporaine pour trois millions d'habitants – 1922" FLC 29712 © FLC; 1997 Artists Rights Society (ARS), New York/ADAGP, Paris/FLC.

Ludwig Karl Hilberseimer, German, 1885–1967, Hochhausstadt (Highrise city): Perspective View, East-West Street, ink and watercolor on paper, 1924, 96.5 x 148 cm. Gift of George E. Danforth, 1983.991. Photograph © 1996, The Art Institute of Chicago, All Rights Reserved.

This edition published in 1998 in the United States of America by Westview Press, 5500 Central Avenue, Boulder, Colorado 80301-2877

First published in hardcover in 1997 by Basic Books

Page design by Andrew Smith.
Page composition by Joseph Gisini/Andrew Smith Graphics, Inc.

A CIP catalog record for this book is available from the Library of Congress.
ISBN 0-8133-3545-0

The paper used in this publication meets the requirements of the American National Standard for Permanence of Paper for Printed Library Materials Z39.48-1984.

10   9   8   7   6   5   4   3   2

FREE

Contents

Acknowledgments

This book has been enriched by the advice and criticism offered by several friends and colleagues. In particular, I want to thank Nat Glazer, Joseph Koerner, Marty Peretz, Peter G. Rowe, Witold Rybczynski, Michael Sorkin, and Leon Wieseltier, who read the manuscript and made invaluable suggestions. My thanks also to Jack Stoddart, Angel Guerra, and Lynne Missen, our editor, all at Stoddart Publishing, for their encouragement and support; to everyone at Basic Books; to Linda Kahn; and to Elsa Franklin, whose belief in the book led to its joint publication in the United States and Canada.

Wendy Kohn began working with me on this book in 1993 as a researcher and editor. As time went by, it became apparent that her contribution extended well beyond that of editor. I am particularly grateful for her insistence that no urban proposals relevant to North America can overlook the power of the American dream of dispersal and openness, and that contemporary concepts must therefore reconcile the forces of concentration and dispersal.

MOSHE SAFDIE
CAMBRIDGE, MASSACHUSETTS
MARCH 1997

Prologue

In 1959, as a graduating student from McGill architecture school in Montreal, I set out on a study trip sponsored by the Canadian Central Mortgage and Housing corporation. Five students, one from each of the five architecture schools in the country, we traveled through the suburbs and downtowns of American and Canadian cities at the height of the suburban explosion. Having moved to Montreal from Israel only a few years earlier, I relished this eight-week voyage as my first true exposure to the North American pattern of urbanization that seemed to be leading the way for the rest of the world.

Traveling from the dense Northeast to the Midwest and West coast, I found myself repeatedly and profoundly impressed by the force of suburbanization — the desire for dispersal outward from city after city, and the ubiquitous dream of individually owning one's house and garden. Yet all five of us were particularly charmed by our visits to downtown San Francisco, Georgetown in Washington, DC, and Rittenhouse Square in Philadelphia. The attached, compact buildings stepping up the hills in San Francisco, the brick houses lining the streets of Georgetown, and the elegant, well-defined urban square in Philadelphia were all reminders of the vitality of places where people of diverse backgrounds mingled, of the idealized image of cities we each carried in our mind's eye. These places convinced us of the merits of traditional urbanity, and the necessity for its revitalization.

In contrast was the inhuman and monotonous stacking of people in high-rise buildings — mostly public housing projects — in and around central cities. And even then, you could already see the emerging replacements for our once grand and vital urbanity: the great malls in the suburbs, the endless highway strips, and the winding streets of identical single-family houses. It seemed to me that urbanism's darkest hour was upon us: with the affluent escaping to the suburbs, poverty and dilapidation were coming to dominate most of downtown.

At the time, I was coming to realize the paradox of contemporary urbanism: the dream of a home and garden that are distant from the ills of the city *alongside* a desire for the vitality of downtown. I translated this paradox into an architectural challenge: to invent a building type that provided the lifestyle of a house with a garden, but that was compact enough to be constructed in the central city. This way, you could have your cake and eat it too, I thought — live within reach of the vital center *and* enjoy the amenities of a suburban house.

"For everyone a garden" was the way I phrased this goal for myself, the inspiration for a new type of urban living. Returning to McGill, I canceled my earlier plan to design the Israeli Knesset as my thesis project and instead proposed a project to develop a new concept for urban housing. I began constructing large models out of Lego, stacking plastic blocks representing houses one on top of the other, each one forming a roof garden for the unit above. Experimenting with various patterns, I built frames in which the houses were suspended, and sketched out traditional shop-lined streets both on the ground and in the air. This was to lead two years later to Habitat '67, a project I designed and constructed as part of the 1967 world's fair in Montreal.

Habitat, as built, focused on the tension between single-family houses and high-rise apartment buildings: if people could have a house with a garden in the city center, I thought, they might no longer feel compelled to leave the city for the suburbs. The project was as dense as traditional apartment buildings, yet provided gardens, privacy, and individual identity. I believed this design strategy might become a model as a remedy for the inhuman conditions of high-rise public housing complexes, as well as for "luxury" housing in the city.

Three decades later, I realize that by reducing it to purely architectural terms, I had misunderstood the paradox of the contemporary city. During the 1960s, we architects felt we could make a difference: we could influence the character of urban development, revitalize downtowns, and stabilize suburban sprawl. We continued to think of the city in traditional historical terms, with a cohesive center surrounded by suburbs — a radiating pattern of density and intensity set within a rural region — and focused primarily on the meaning of, and the need for, the traditional downtown. Could the affluent who had left over the previous two decades be convinced to live there again? Could civic institutions be revitalized and strengthened? Could the slums be rehabilitated, or should they be replaced?

These interests were not primarily altruistic on the part of architects. Rather, the business and intellectual communities understood at the time that the whole urban environment could not function with a rotten core. It was simply assumed that the functioning of contemporary society depended on what I have come to term "interactive centers," consolidated places for urban life. Yet while architects, intellectuals, and politicians discussed these issues, suburbanization only intensified.

We now recognize that the fundamental problems of the past decades represent complex economic and technological trends that have ushered in a way of life. And that desire to escape the city involved the social as well as the physical. It was loaded with the implicit wish for the comfort of living with "your own kind" — insulated from the poverty, dirt, and diverse populations associated with urban life. Therefore, clearly, preserving the richness of the city center alongside the freedom of the suburbs cannot be accomplished by "merely" inventing new building types. To "have our cake and eat it too" means recognizing not only what our urban landscape has come to look like, but what forces shape it and how they operate.

If we look at cities over the past century, we can see that each transformation in urban form has been linked with some type of transportation revolution: electric streetcars spawned the early suburban towns; elevators begat tall buildings. And the automobile, of course, burst all boundaries, scattering new, low-density development across the countryside. Like many revolutions, the causes and certainly the effects of this transformation have been poorly understood.

Today, ideas about the relationship of transportation systems to cities and suburbs, urban form, organization, and building types remain vague and outdated. We continue to formulate policy and generate technology based on lifestyles and concepts of the built environment that are already many decades old, never to be regained. As we continue to build and shape our cities, the question must be asked, What might the next transportation revolution be, and how will it affect our lives? What about the city after the automobile?

PART I

VISIONS OF THE CITY

CHAPTER 1

The Ailing City

Universal Dispersal

There is a consensus today that our cities are not well. Toward the end of the twentieth century, they are inundated with problems — physical, social, and economic. Urban transportation is deficient; inner city problems have deepened; violent crime remains a serious threat in vast areas of the historic city centers.

Is there a common denominator to the ailments of cities of the industrialized West and of the populous Third World, in the North and in the Tropics — of New York and Mexico City, Jakarta and Hong Kong, Toronto and Copenhagen? Despite distinct differences of scale and resources, of climate and history, there is, indeed, a universal pattern. Everywhere in the world we find examples of expanded regional cities — cities that in recent decades have burst out of their traditional boundaries, urbanizing and suburbanizing entire regions, and housing close to a third of the world's population.[1]

The initial explosion of the traditional city was primarily generated by industrial-era population growth due to prosperity, better medicine, immigration, and the shrinking of traditional agricultural economies, which sent workers streaming into cities. Movement to suburbs surrounding the urban core was then facilitated by extended transit and rail lines, and finally, most decisively, by the automobile. In the United States, the most intensive growth occurred after the Second World War and was enhanced by the construction of the interstate highway system, funded by federal legislation in 1956. In 1940, cars were owned by about one person in five[2]; today, we are fast approaching an equal population of cars and people.

Automobiles and their road systems have completely redefined the old boundaries of cities. Today's regional city of seventy or eighty miles across encompasses the "old" downtown (or in some cases, several old downtowns), as well as industrial, commercial, and residential sprawl. As seen from the air, urbanization extends for miles beyond the old centers, clustering haphazardly along the freeway system and thickening around its cloverleaf intersections. From this distance, in fact, the car and the freeway have become the essence of the regional city.

Infrastructure Misfit

There are many conflicting views as to the impact and meaning of the exploded city in our lives. But without exception, all agree on one issue: a fundamental conflict — a misfit — exists between the scale of cities and the transportation systems that serve them. Dispersed around the region, we can no longer conform our individual paths of travel to the fixed lines of mass transit. And the more highways and expressways we build, the sooner they become overburdened with traffic; no investment in highways seems great enough to satisfy our voracious necessity to travel by car.

The automobile has devastated the physical fabric of both older and younger cities. Older cities have had to adapt their downtowns to traffic volumes unimagined at the time they were built. In these cities, which were originally served by streetcars, streets evolved with buildings lining the sidewalks, providing elaborate window shopping and ceremonious entrances for the pedestrian; together, buildings defined streets and public spaces.

Neither the scale of traditional streets, nor the size of individual building parcels, anticipated the growing volume of traffic or the need for off-street parking. Common solutions to making older cities accessible to cars have been widening streets (Montreal's Boulevard René Lévesque); displacing pedestrians to underground districts (Montreal; Toronto) or overhead walkways (Minneapolis); cutting new traffic arteries between neighboring urban districts (Seattle's waterfront; Boston's North End; downtown Hartford, CT) or through the middle of cohesive neighborhoods (everywhere); and replacing fine old urban buildings with parking lots all over the world. As the highways have taken over, the tightly woven fabric of urban streets has been progressively destroyed.

In newer North American cities, the patterns of development, land-use, and land coverage were all determined by the requirements and presumptions of car-dominated transportation from the beginning of their major growth. Each new act of city building required appropriate parking to be included at the outset, and wide urban streets were laid out and constructed with the specific goal of assuring car access. Buildings, the distances between them, and the sequences of entering and exiting them all deferred to the demands of the car. The result was an unprecedented scale and pattern: large amounts of paved open space devoted primarily to roadways and parking, with structures interspersed at distances. Every physical premise of the traditional city disappeared: continuous pedestrian circulation; a well-defined and habitable public domain; and the entire array of architectural details on buildings and streets — door frames, entry moldings, window sills, stoops, lamps, benches, trees, and all. The new form addressed the issue of vehicular access and parking, but did not replace or reinvent other aspects of urban life that had been inscribed into the older city grid over its history.

The vast majority of development in cities such as Los Angeles, Dallas, and Houston, for example, is dispersed over a region of four to six thousand square miles[3] in a pattern not related to any type of pedestrian travel, but generated instead by regional highways and their principal intersections, and extended by regional arterial and county roads. With this dispersal has emerged both new building types and entirely new urban forms: the "strip," an arterial road lined with readily available parking and low-density, one-story commercial development; the mall or regional shopping center, a concentration of stores surrounded by a sea of parking and generally located on a freeway intersection; and the suburban office complex, one huge block or cluster of buildings set along a regional highway, served by a parking structure or enormous lots.

The highway has come to double as a new kind of urban street. Along these vast thoroughfares, no order of principal urban streets and public buildings exists like those that structure cities like Manhattan or Washington, DC. Highways separate office parks from shopping centers, which are separated from hotels and housing. Schools are isolated in residential suburbs, distant from cultural and recreation facilities that remain in the traditional centers. The distinguishing pattern of dispersed land uses is not a composition, but an *isolation* of different activities.

How have we reacted to this reign of the car? City governments have legislated requirements for ample parking in urban centers only to give up in despair, as more parking only attracts more cars, and then requires even more parking. The alternative policy, to forbid the construction of parking, aims to send commuters back to public transportation and carpooling. But while billions have been invested in subways and other urban mass transportation with some positive results (Toronto, Montreal, San Francisco, and Washington, DC), the process is often long, embattled, and immensely political. And attempts to do so in the newer automobile-era cities — Los Angeles, Dallas, Houston, Denver — often fail or are stalled because of greatly dispersed and random travel patterns, few continuous preexisting rights-of-way, and the absence of sufficiently concentrated populations.

Canada has struggled to keep its passenger train system intact, while failing to improve technology (and speed) and making no attempt to address the heavily traveled, longer-distance routes like the Montreal–Ottawa–Toronto corridor. Congestion at airports in such areas — on the roads leading to them and in the air itself — has suggested to many planners that rapid public transportation serving a region of three to four hundred miles could help alleviate the congestion associated with air travel. Yet despite the example of heavily government-subsidized rail systems built in Japan, France, and several other European countries, until very recently there has been little investment or hope of success for such rapid rail systems in North America.

But if neither more highways and cars, nor more subway lines and rapid rail as we know them today seem to fit our needs, then we either have to alter living habits that have matured over a century, or reconsider the transportation infrastructure so essential to supporting our mobile lives. In either case, we face a profound poverty of vision in planning for our cities.

The Time Is Now

Today's indiscriminate dispersal — the spatial separation of almost every type of new construction — is the product of the better part of a century's policy of laissez-faire land-use planning. In an era when market forces have been trusted to satisfy all worthwhile considerations, dispersed development has appeared not merely inevitable, but efficient and responsive to society's will. Yet our current environment clearly fails to satisfy many of our most urgent and basic needs. Never in recent history have we heard in the popular press so many calls to rebuild "community"; to create neighborhoods in which we can walk; to control car-related pollution; and to conserve our dwindling stretches of natural landscape. But any proposal to create sustained, vital urbanism today cannot be achieved for the majority of urban dwellers without an understanding of, and a confrontation with, the real, complex, and competing forces that have for decades so universally threatened our cities.

This book focuses on what these forces are, how they act destructively, and how we might take control of current patterns. Forty-three percent of the world's 5.5 billion inhabitants live in cities, many of them regional mega-cities, which are growing recklessly, increasing in congestion, and daily threatening their environment and its resources. If we are to progress, we must take lessons from the mega-city, not the Italian hill town, nor the American pre-industrial village. We must study the airport, the mega-mall, the convention centers, the enormous parking lots and structures, the freeways and their interchanges — even the sprawling strip developments along highways — for an understanding of current needs, contemporary behavior, and real economic necessities. We need not accept, but we must understand the powerful patterns that shape the city today.

Some say that mild massaging can make today's city workable. But surely the moment has come to declare "time out" — a pause, please, for reflection and assessment. Why have the old programs and investment in the prevailing patterns not worked? Why has the new expanded city failed to satisfy many of our needs for beauty, affiliation, or social commitment? How can we, as a society, begin to take responsibility not only for solving the problems we have already created, but also for planning to realize our dreams for the future?

In order to go forward and consider the city that might be, we must look at the many visions of our cities since the beginning of the massive urbanization that marks this century. What have the proposals been? Have they been tested, and if so, what have we learned from them? What were the values that guided their authors, and to what extent has society *itself* changed in the unfolding of the saga of twentieth-century urbanism?

CHAPTER 2

The Evolving City

Hierarchical City

Alexander the Great traveled the plains of Asia in the fourth century BC, determined to build a series of grand, new cities. As sites were selected, a generic plan was adapted to the particular features — the hills, rivers, waterfronts — of each site. Two monumental streets, the Cardo and the Decumanus, were laid out to cross each town east–west and north–south, from gate to gate. Major public buildings, theaters, palaces, gymnasia, markets, and temples were strategically placed along these principal routes. The royal administration saw to it that the main streets and public buildings along them were designed with enough formality and cohesion that altogether they formed a harmonious assemblage befitting a royal city. Individuals, on the other hand, were responsible for building the smaller-scale residential fabric of houses and workshops, extending out to the city walls.

Through all Greek and Roman cities, this idea of a monumental spine forming the central lifeline of a city persisted. Byzantine Jerusalem, as described in the Madaba mosaic plan, is a vivid illustration of the principle. The walled city is punctuated by the city gates, which are the points of principal entry, and the Cardo Maximus, a sixty-five-foot-wide colonnaded street, stretches north–south, between two main gates. The

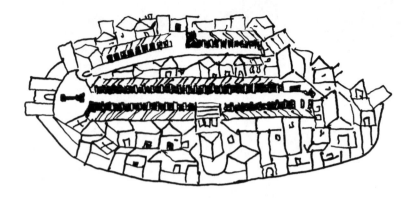

Madaba plan of Byzantine Jerusalem

Decumanus crosses at a ninety-degree angle from gate to temple in the east–west direction. The Holy Sepulcher, the palaces, the markets, and places of culture are all located along the Cardo. To this day, even with layer after layer of the city rebuilt over seventeen centuries, the same organization remains.

In the centuries preceding our own, from Pope Sixtus V's sixteenth-century axial plan for Rome to the grand nineteenth-century schemes for Vienna and Paris, the public domain was the combination of principal streets or boulevards designated as important ceremonial and commercial axes, and piazzas and public buildings as focal points or formal enclosures. This model of a hierarchical city, in which the public domain and its public buildings form spines or districts through the general fabric of urban development, has produced vital places with a clear sense of orientation and legibility.

Urban historian Spiro Kostof defines pre-automobile cities as "places where a certain energized crowding of people" took place.[1] Historical cities provided intense and active meeting places for commerce, the exchange of ideas, worship, and recreation. Even dictatorships produced a wide variety of spaces

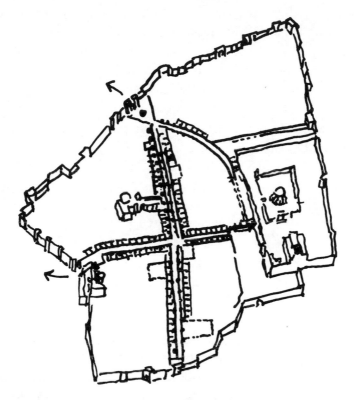

Plan of the Old City of Jerusalem today

for formal and informal public gathering. People of diverse backgrounds came to, and lived in, the city, knowing that this conglomeration of people and the interaction offered by it would enrich their lives.

The Modern City
At the turn of the twentieth century, during a period of unprecedented urban population growth, industrialization, and then crowding and filth — now familiar faults of industrial cities — there occurred a breakdown of many of the traditional urban

systems of hierarchy and scale. At the moment, it seemed to those contemplating the future that the advent of automobiles, highways, and high-rise construction would provide an escape from the limitations and some of the oppressions of the old compact city. Greater speeds and heights held out the promise of breaking boundaries of all sorts, and, throughout the early decades of the century, inspired numerous explorations for a new kind of city.

Turn-of-the-century visionaries offered divergent recipes for the future city, and their attitudes toward density and urbanity varied enormously. Ebenezer Howard's influential "Garden City" proposal of 1898 suggested a city of dispersed low-density residential settlements. With parks at their center and agriculture at their periphery, the communities of Howard's vision appealed to those in England who still associated urban concentration with the "dark Satanic mills" (in William Blake's famous words) of the Industrial Revolution. And for the many Americans who were troubled by the influx into cities of unskilled labor from the South and new immigrants from Europe, and thus eager to distance their family lives from the hub of economic activity, the idea of living in a distant house set in nature was alluring — and, in hindsight, was a clear, early spark to the later suburban explosion.

Three decades later, Frank Lloyd Wright also resisted the idea of dense and concentrated cities. In fact, "to decentralize," he believed, was one of "several inherently just rights of man."[2] His proposal for Broadacre City, a theoretical American suburban–regional city first exhibited in 1935, presented a uniform scattering of buildings across the land to satisfy this "inherent right." Small, decentralized commercial town centers — each one spatially distinct — would stand adjacent to every residential neighborhood. Like Ebenezer Howard before him, Wright assumed that these suburban cities would generate primarily local traffic, and would remain relatively autonomous and self-sufficient as communities.

Yet at the level of realistic transportation solutions, Wright's proposal broke down entirely, even at the time it was designed. In his vision, "every Broadacre citizen has his own car. Multiple-lane highways make travel safe and enjoyable. The road system and construction is such that no signals nor any lamp-posts need be seen."[3] In many ways Broadacre City anticipated the new automobile cities that have emerged in the American West, Southwest, and around the older cities of the East, while totally underestimating the traffic volumes they would generate.

Like many other visions of the time, Broadacre City includes at least some form of high-rise tower. Its towers are dispersed around the landscape in the manner of visual landmarks, as places of work, with no discernible parking lots or parking structures. While Broadacre City does include small parking areas at the neighborhood shopping centers, could Wright have meant his office workers to commute by foot?

Wright's underestimation of the traffic congestion ultimately caused by a suburban lifestyle becomes more understandable when we learn that his city's intended population was only seven thousand. Wright did not come close to anticipating our regional populations of tens of millions, with residents traveling many miles each day to two jobs per household — to schools, hospitals, recreation centers, cultural events, and more. But Wright did imagine that with Broadacre City in place, "the ghastly heritage left by overcrowding in overdone ultra-capitalistic centers would be likely to disappear in three or four generations."[4] And after nearly five decades of suburbanization and years of declining city centers, we can only lament that in this dream he was prophetic.

In both North America and Europe, however, there were also those who explored ways to adapt the existing intense, interactive, and dense city to the modern era. To this end, the multi-level transportation networks and stacked streets drawn by Harvey Wiley Corbett (1913), the dramatic and elegant New York cityscapes of Hugh Ferriss (1930s), as well as the many set designs for Fritz Lang's film, *Metropolis* (1927), remain even today vividly persuasive. In a spirit and mood of radical restructuring, the answer for the more socially idealistic architects and planners was a reinterpretation of urbanity itself. Many European urban visions, in particular, appreciated both the opportunity and the necessity for concentration, from Camillo Sitte's humane and idiosyncratic cities in *Der Städtebau* (*City Building*, 1889) to Antonio Sant'Elia's energetic, mixed-use city, the *Città Nuova* (*New City*, 1914), and Le Corbusier's expansive, towering *Ville Radieuse* (*Radiating City*, 1930). But each of these visions differed over the form concentration might take — and from them we inherited theories of both low- and high-rise concentration, *and* low- and high-rise dispersal.

View of stacked streets by Corbett

Le Corbusier, for example, imagined a city set free in greenery — ordered towers served by vast highways, but standing in a park. While seeking to erase the ills of the compact city, Le Corbusier valued the density achieved by skyscrapers. His *Cité de Trois Milles* (1922) and its adaptation to central Paris, the *Plan Voisin* (1925), replace the traditional seven-story urban fabric of Paris with a grid of giant towers that are "deconcentrated" across the open landscape. On one side of his drawings for the *Plan Voisin* stands traditional Paris with its medieval streets and grand boulevards; on the other, undifferentiated open space marked by identical freestanding office towers and mid-rise apartment buildings. The high-rise, ordered sprawl in Le Corbusier's schemes was such a radical break from traditional urbanity, and differs so strongly from the eventual dispersed low-rise suburbs, that it suggests an environment it is tempting to call "dis-urbanized."

By the time post-war reconstruction began, the concept of an open city of towers set "free" in the landscape had taken hold of the minds of planners, architects, and the public. But as these earlier modernist, utopian visions were concretely realized, disappointment set in. Some, more cynical, considered the results as evidence of a grand deception: drawings and descriptions of towers in the park had not adequately conveyed the void that would be created by the acres of parking, endless configurations of highways, and undistinguished spaces that were beginning to appear on urban peripheries and centers alike. In reality, the green of the drawings became gray as the parks became asphalt. The result of this visionary concept was a flat connective fabric of highway and parking lot.

Perhaps the most surprising realization and shock about the shortcomings of the utopian models was that they defied and defeated one of the original purposes of urbanity itself — to facilitate interaction among people. While individual buildings had once combined to form outdoor collective spaces, in the new models, there were no collective spaces planned or replaced by any other forum for interaction. Not only did Le Corbusier fail to reconcile the scale, mass, and concentrated activities represented by the tall buildings with any new idea of urban connectivity, *he did not even try.*

"The street wears us out. It is altogether disgusting!" exclaimed Le Corbusier at the time. "Why, then, does it still exist?"[5] he asked, evidently with the agreement of such figures as Ludwig Hilberseimer and the other major players in the Congrès Internationaux d'Architecture Moderne (CIAM), as they met throughout the 1930s and projected images of cities devoid of any element to compose the parts into a whole — any compelling image of what the *meeting places* of a new city should be.

In the *City of Tomorrow* (1929) Le Corbusier wrote, "The center of the great city is like a funnel into which every street shoots its traffic . . .," and concluded that "wide avenues must be driven through the centers of our towns," presaging countless

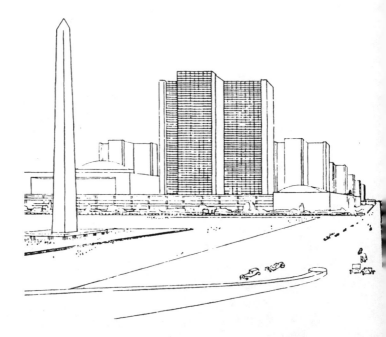

downtown highway projects carved right out of the historic meeting places of busy streets, commerce, and civic institutions. "We must create vast and sheltered public parking places where cars can be left during working hours,"[6] he suggested, enthusiastically describing one of the most widespread and drastic influences on the shape of cities for years to come.

It took the passing of a full generation before a new group of younger architects, known as "Team 10," came to appreciate that the Modern movement had entirely overlooked what had been a fundamental component of urban life: the pedestrian precinct. As they took stock of the post–Second World War cities, they saw scores of new developments in Europe and North America constructed under the influence of the proposals of the 1930s that had been deprived of a public domain.

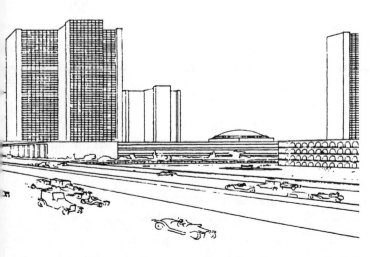

View of a contemporary city by Le Corbusier

Indeed, for Team 10, the pedestrian was the most important component of the city. Team 10 architects were also interested in harmony and continuity between existing and new development. Whereas Le Corbusier had envisioned drastic ruptures between the historic fabric of Paris and his own freestanding towers, Aldo Van Eyck, Giancarlo De Carlo, and other Team 10 designers wove architectural tapestries that attempted to reinstate a place for the pedestrian in the city and to create some consonance between the old and new.

But while Team 10 met and exchanged polemics, major new satellite towns, neighborhoods, and public housing projects in reconstructed Germany, France, and the outskirts of cities all over North America effectively realized the earlier dream of towers in the "park." By the 1960s, a flight over major European and American cities already revealed long stretches of this new kind of place.

Le Corbusier's vision is commonplace in every contemporary city today. Yet, ironically, we can see that even Le Corbusier and his colleagues underestimated and misunderstood the impact that the automobile would have on urban form. Even with the original modernist emphasis on grand networks of highways, roads, parking lots, and parking structures, the effect of all this automobile infrastructure was simply beyond anyone's frame of vision at the time. It is as if the modernists allowed the city to be designed by the will of the car, only to discover, decades later, that its will was rather different from what they had anticipated.

Contemporary City

The enormous European reconstruction effort after the Second World War, large-scale development in the post-colonial world, and American affluence assured that modernist urbanism was built around the globe, and both architects and the public were affected profoundly. For their part, the public (as well as politicians) began to suspect the *Brave New World* design solutions that had promised to improve the welfare of humanity. Not only were these places often disappointing, but their importance seemed diminished by the reality of poverty, hunger, and loss around them. In this context, it became only natural for the design professions to retreat from megalomania and recognize the limits on their own ability to influence and change the way people lived.

By the 1970s, the role of architects in creating a vision for cities had entirely shifted, and the retreat in mainstream architectural thinking became institutionalized in academia. At Harvard, following decades of close association between environmental, political, and architectural issues under Walter Gropius and Josep Lluis Sert, the university decided that study and training in architecture and urban policy did not belong together. City planning, now understood primarily as the making of policy, was incorporated into the Kennedy School of Government. Architecture, landscape architecture, and urban design (now understood as the physical design of urban districts, with limited consideration of political, social, and economic factors), remained in the Design School, "purified" of the mundane and "elevated" to the status of Art.

Within a decade, the isolated pursuit of architectural form had become both plausible and respectable in schools and in practice. Architects had withdrawn from the "vision of the city business" and retreated to the simpler world of form-making at the scale of the building alone. And a climate developed in which the expression and comment of an individual architect became more important in the design of buildings than perceiving the city as a whole and architecture as collective, connective, or shared.

The thrust of much recent work has been to refrain from full participation: to consider any area outside a given building lot as beyond the sphere of an architect's influence. With the city thus out of bounds, many architects have for the past fifteen years concentrated only on single buildings or self-contained complexes. By emphasizing primarily the personal and the individual, architectural ideas can thus be developed without any particular acknowledgment of the conflicting and constraining forces of the economy, social policy, and what often appear to be overwhelming related transportation problems.

This is not to say that architects have stopped acknowledging the city completely. As always, there exist both conservative and radical schools of thought on the subject. The conservative school has come to be associated with neo-traditionalism, "New Urbanism," as well as the architectural crusade of His Royal Highness Prince Charles of England. For the past decade, the Prince has been an articulate critic of the ills of modernism — not so much of the modernist vision, but of the tangible results in the field. He has lamented the discontinuity between existing historic cities and the new mega-buildings of today; the devastation caused to traditional cities by contemporary transportation; the congestion and density of high-rise centers; the huge scale of places like Canary Wharf in comparison with the pedestrianized, and in the Prince's view, more "dignified" cities of the nineteenth century. The Prince's observations are supported by more specific architectural schemes intending to show that the humanity, charm, and the good life of nineteenth-century towns and cities can be recreated, and to this end, the ideas of the architect and adviser to the Prince of Wales, Leon Krier, and his brother Rob Krier, have been compelling.

In the United States, an interest in turning back the urbanistic clock began to gather particular momentum in the early

1990s, as the end of the 1980s' economic boom halted years of intense and widespread development. In a climate of scaled-back development aspirations, the firm Duany Plater-Zyberk of Miami began working with land developers to counteract the decades-old zoning laws of the automobile suburbs, which had established easy vehicular circulation as the preeminent concern in laying out new development. Their seashore resort of Seaside, Florida, is emblematic of their goals. The development was designed around a small town center, with streets and sidewalks scaled to the pedestrian, and the car largely confined to alley-ways. Built in a traditional vernacular style of shuttered clapboard houses with porches, the development echoes pre-automobile villages like colonial Williamsburg, Sturbridge, or the port town of Nantucket.

This is no accident. The planners who subscribe to the values of the self-named group of New Urbanists have expressed their goal as a return to the "compact, close-knit community" they present as "a cherished American icon."[7] Delicate in their scale, many of these projects constitute appealing designs for suburban enclaves, critiques of the typical 1960s suburban tract development. However, these schemes seem to deny the existence of conditions commonplace to any city. They are visually described without any hint of the presence of the building types we associate with industry, commerce, and business, without even the attempt to acknowledge the number of cars or the volume of parking we realistically need (and want). At least visually, most of these proposals remain suspiciously aloof from the primary economic, social, and technological forces shaping urban life.

At the opposite end of the spectrum, and at times even dismissed as science fiction, are the radical visions of the city that might be. In the 1960s these were manifested in proposals of complex, three-dimensional high-rise arrangements served by a network of connecting tubes, as in the work of the Archigram group. More recently, there have been proposals of urbanistic "landscapes." Architect Michael Sorkin, for example, has developed intricate three-dimensional proposals in which building-like forms extend vertically and horizontally, inclined and cantilevered, their shapes inspired by bridges or aqueducts. Transportation corridors at ground level and building masses in the air are generated by either multiple geometries, or no perceptible order at all. Inventive, exciting, and full of energy, these proposals in general completely displace the car as the primary mode of transportation in favor of a variety of some-what mysterious systems. Here we see not the rejection of density and intensity, but its celebration — not exactly ignoring the exis-tence of the car, but leaping forward to its obsolescence, envisioning a society whose interactive needs are amplified and expanded as compared with today.

Of all those speculating on the future of urban form, archi-tect Rem Koolhaas has emerged as a most acute observer and supporter of cities, driven by his conviction that we are head-ing toward "a definitive, global 'triumph' of the urban condition."[8] In his writings, he indicts the Modern movement's abstract architectural goals and repetitive, simplistic urbanism for causing decades of urban destruction. Further, he recognizes the depth of the public's distrust of these failed mechanisms for endowing cities with cohesiveness, order, and harmony.

Yet Koolhaas believes the chaotic assemblages of build-ing, infrastructure, transportation, unbuilt land, and landscape that represent much of our current environment are inevitable — an expression of society's needs and desires. A new urban-ism, he believes, should abandon "pretensions of harmony and overall coherence" entirely. Following his own advice, Koolhaas has described a set of his urban projects in general as "celebrat[ing] the end of sentimentality," and specifically, as dealing with "nothingness." [9]

In the spectrum of proposals for the city, there are thus the "humanists" at one end, with a desire to preserve, or in most cases to replicate, traditionally "comfortable" formal values in the environment; a sense of personal identity; and the gentility of life in a small town. At the other end, there are those who believe we face a new kind of reality that requires architectural expression, precludes looking backward, or renders traditional communities entirely obsolete and thus, irrelevant to society today.

At both ends of this spectrum, there are thought-provoking answers to important problems. We must, with the conservatives, strive to reestablish qualities of scale and space that relate to the human body. With the more radical, we must recognize that we cannot solve today's challenges as we did yesterday. But we cannot "go with the flow." There is a wide gap between what we see when we look at our cities, and what we get when we try to accept any of the current proposals as a comprehensive solution.

As we move into the twenty-first century, we see changes in the technology of communications and information transfer that threaten to replace the very necessity for personal contact. The shift in jobs over several decades from manufacturing toward service and the more recent growth of entrepreneurial cybernetics continue to lure workplaces from downtowns to regional locations accessible only by car. The deepening spatial segregation of the poor and the affluent has had drastic consequences upon the opportunities and education available to vast numbers of people. Our natural resources have been so burdened and damaged by the prevailing urban patterns that we have witnessed a global cry of alarm.

The form and shape of the city and the quality of life it offers is a synthesis of all these economic, technological, demographic, and environmental factors. They are so interdependent and intertwined that many claim the futility of attempting any restructuring at all. But each of these shifts inevitably reverberates through our daily *physical* patterns of living. Whether we will guide their effects and satisfy new demands, or simply announce chance successes and catastrophes as they happen, the choice is ours.

CHAPTER 3

The End of the City

Why should we continue to think about vital, interactive cities today? Why not accept the consequences of the evolving dispersed city as desirable, simply on the logic that a million individual decisions have added up to one broad societal decision to abandon intense urbanism?

To many, the dispersed city *is* the future, fulfilling the dreams of millions of people. Rising on the urban peripheries of Washington, DC, Chicago, Toronto, Vancouver, Los Angeles, and Dallas, millions of square feet of office parks, high-tech industrial plants, shopping malls, suburban housing tracts, and hotels extend along America's highways. These places have been described with excitement as a "New Frontier"[1] by author Joel Garreau, and as "multitudes of experimental communities of tomorrow"[2] by theorist Edward Soja. If these new "Edge Cities," as Garreau has argued, will soon be entirely self-sufficient, and if, as Soja describes, these are the incubation places for tomorrow's environment, then striving to maintain and foster the interactive downtown is of secondary importance. If jobs, culture, education, medical care, and shopping are provided effectively and richly in these new Edge Cities, why then bother with the center? Congested, often dilapidated, a concentration of economic pathologies, the historic core might best be abandoned, or at least pushed to the sidelines as a priority.

With great distances now built between us, some have eloquently made the case that the era of the interactive city, whose inherent purpose was face-to-face human contact, has come to an end.

Cybernetic Dispersal

In the Western world, the exchange of goods and information is swiftly moving from the traditional web of streets to the immaterial web of electronics. The function of the great, vital marketplace will, in the next few decades, be challenged by interactive home shopping and an array of other electronic merchandising techniques. Concerts, operas, plays, and films have been appreciated televisually for decades. Collaboration among multi-disciplinary groups in business, industry, and the sciences will be handled by e-mail, the Worldwide Web, teleconferencing, and "telepresence"[3] — virtual presence by video telephone. Served by almost unlimited venues for electronic interaction, institutions and individuals could thus neatly spread around the globe.

In this new environment, we might have a universal scattering of millions of villages, giving individuals locally the comforts of village-scale life and electronically the cultural richness of great historic cities. In time, trips might be undertaken for pleasure, recreation, and occasionally business, but the routine, daily commute that burdens so many would disappear entirely. For creative exchange, we might emerge several times a year from our own village to travel to a truly urban center. Like a modern-day conference center or theme park served by hotels, the objective could be, for example, profound — to participate in medical research; pragmatic — to sell one's product; or entertaining — to enjoy one's culture. In such a world, people might travel to highly specialized complexes, convention centers, and trade marts for business exchanges. They might attend conferences and think-tanks for brainstorming. For a week at a time, they might participate in cultural and music festivals with the live presentation of plays, operas, and movies. To offer children lessons in history, science, and civic involvement, there might even be special theme parks for both entertainment and education.

There is, however, a nagging question about this model. When we go to the place of festivals to enjoy plays, operas, and concerts, we might wonder how these creative products were composed and written and produced. As surgeons become able to advise on operations remotely, as more teachers and managers are able to project their digital presence across the globe, and as writers, directors, artists, and musicians together gain entry into the virtual practice halls of cyberspace, will each one no longer rely on the energy, inspiration, and stimulation of human contact? Within a network of electronic culture, where will the place for creative, face-to-face collaboration be?

The Case for Interactive Centers

Civilization has long been characterized by the ever-increasing specialization of the roles people have played in society and the fields of knowledge they have pursued. Twenty centuries ago, ancient Rome offered a setting in which concentrations of expertise could be developed, and its citizens thrived on the fruits of specialization. Depth of knowledge was believed to depend upon breadth of exposure, and at its height around the second century BC, the Roman Forum functioned as the place where groups of skilled craftspeople and scholars, politicians, and preparers of food could all congregate.[4] The built forms of the city (the processional routes, broad squares, and the Forum with its monumental buildings) encouraged interaction among all segments of society and supported a civic culture of public games, festivals, and cyclical religious rituals.

The origin of early cities and their later evolution was, in fact, based on the need for places of interactive exchange: the marketplace, the government, and the spiritual and intellectual centers. When people walked through the city, by necessity they interacted with others outside their own social and professional spheres. Urban life broke down social barriers, as a wide range of business, commercial, cultural, and educational exchanges occurred within a single zone — the downtown center, which included formal public meeting places, as well as informal venues like cafes and arcades, crowded streets and parks.

Now as our roles in society become ever more specialized (and thus more isolating), our basic need for interaction increases. Major contemporary hospitals are concentrations into a single complex of the hundreds of specialists who have become essential in providing the full array of medical services. The great research labs — NASA, the Superconducting Super Collider Laboratory, cancer, AIDS, and genetic research centers — are each examples of the new mode of "super-mind" made possible by the collective interaction of many individual minds, each highly skilled in an increasingly narrow spectrum of knowledge. The disciplinary generalists — the designers, writers, artists, and philosophers — then remain as catalysts for these mega-projects, synthesizing long-term objectives with their own sense of perspective, yet totally dependent on the specialists for their expertise.

As digital modes of communication expand, the need for physical proximity appears to increase as well. Today most professions seem to be continuously inventing new modes for personal interaction: annual, semi-annual, and even more frequent conferences, conventions, exhibits. Hotel complexes mushroom around major national airports, sustaining their business not on the transfer passenger who has missed a connection, but primarily on the teams of people coming together for working sessions in the same physical space, and dispersing again to communicate electronically until the next meeting.

In his recent book, *City of Bits*, William J. Mitchell describes cyberspace as "a city unrooted to any definite spot on the surface of the earth, shaped by connectivity and bandwidth constraints rather than by accessibility and land values . . . and inhabited by disembodied and fragmented subjects who exist as collections of aliases and agents."[5] In the face of this vision, can anybody question the necessity for perpetuating and nourishing real, built cities of a human scale?

Spontaneous, unplanned, physical interaction is the essential stuff of life: it makes for a better and richer society; it is a healthier setting for the education and maturing of young people; and it is the condition by which conflicts and suspicion are better dissipated. These fundamental beliefs inevitably lead to the conclusion: we must do all in our power to create an urban structure that fosters stimulating and vital interactive centers.

In the manner of the Roman Forum, we have built institutions in societies around the world as specific catalysts for interaction. Great universities were designed to draw together individuals from every field of human endeavor — from medicine and science, the arts and social sciences — into one community. With its graduate schools, academic departments, laboratories, and institutes, the university fosters specialized research and simultaneously constitutes an entire structure devoted specifically to breaking down barriers to collaboration and interaction. Our cities once were, and could again, become such structures.

Urban Fragmentation

Even though excursions to the old downtown are less frequent than they were a generation ago, many historic centers remain the scientific, educational, financial, and cultural focus of their regions. Manhattan, for example, remains the primary cultural provider for the Greater New York area, and a similar concentration of important cultural facilities within the traditional core is found not only, as we would expect, in the older cities of Europe and North America, but also in relatively new cities such as Dallas, Houston, Singapore, and Tel Aviv. But while the traditional city centers today may continue to signify established culture, to many people, they also mean unsafe, dilapidated areas.

In almost every city, crucial sections of originally thriving downtowns are dying. Drained by "white flight," most center cities have been left with concentrated lower-income populations — often more dependent on social services — and therefore substantially eroded tax bases. With the overall reduction of industrial employment, and the relocation of remaining industry to cheaper land on the urban fringe, a needy labor pool has been increasingly isolated from potential jobs. Therefore, social policies, economic patterns, and racial discord have all combined to create deteriorating and increasingly entrenched living conditions within significant portions of the urban centers.

Repairing our ravaged inner cities is, in many ways, beyond the power and responsibility of architects and planners. National debates over welfare, incentives for commercial development, and even illegal immigration all ultimately relate to the ill health of our cities and of their inhabitants. Unlike the conservatives who tend to construe the entire problem as solvable simply by "growing" the economy, liberals often apply programmatic solutions: from encouraging economic investment in areas now nearly devoid of commerce, to tax incentives for the construction of mixed-income housing and rent subsidies, to programs like the Gautreaux Assisted Housing program in Chicago, which give up entirely on the rehabilitation of the most troubled neighborhoods by moving unemployed and struggling residents, family by family, out to healthy suburbs. Yet when it comes to the physical environment, North America has by and large convinced itself to be unconcerned.

Continuing suburbanization helps maintain this status quo, as dispersed cities work to insulate their most politically and financially powerful populations from the neighborhoods of poverty. In Los Angeles, it is easier to forget the desolation of Watts when you are surrounded by the splendor of Belair, than it is in New York to forget the streets of Harlem when surrounded by the street scene of midtown Manhattan. For those who have escaped to the outer suburbs, violence in the streets and urban housing projects become distant, unthreatening phenomena.

The Power of Design

Several generations of planners and architects, however, have pondered what might be done physically to improve life in the dilapidated neighborhoods of poverty. While there is a wide variety of formal patterns for poor neighborhoods across U.S. cities, from low-density streets of two- or three-story detached buildings to stark and isolated high-rise stretches, the areas all consist of ravaged buildings and rotting infrastructure. Some buildings stand empty and boarded up. Others have not received even minimal maintenance in thirty years. Usually residents occupy rented facilities where there is little pride of ownership, and even basic municipal services are substandard and neglected. Garbage accumulates, roads lie in disrepair, shops remain boarded up season after season. The neighborhood is isolated physically and branded visually, often resembling nothing so much as a war zone.

But how much good can physical intervention do? Would an attempt to clean up these places — to apply fresh paint and plaster to crumbling walls, to replace broken windows with new ones, to plant trees, to remove the garbage — have any substantive effect on the neighborhood? Or will such improvement be short term, a brief facelift to camouflage the ailing soul within? Two decades ago, the City of New York proposed painting geraniums and white curtains in the boarded windows of burnt-out buildings lining the freeway. Can the most idealistic among us not judge such a project as naive?

Yet in the urban realm, there is undeniably a connection between appearances and reality. One of the best examples, and greatest ironies, of recent decades has been the coexistence near downtown Boston of the Kennedy Memorial Library on a peninsula jutting into Boston Harbor, adjacent to Columbia Point, once one of the most deteriorated and crime-infested public housing projects in the United States. It was perhaps the symbolic juxtaposition of the Kennedy administration, with all its social hope and compassion, and the desolated housing project next door that finally led to the funding of a major neighborhood rehabilitation project. Some buildings were gutted and fixed up. Some were reduced in height and new townhouses built to define the streets. Pathways and thoroughfares replaced the anonymous open space between buildings. The whole urban structure was changed.

But the operation was not purely physical. The city approved a proposal to combine a new mix of residents — both renters and owners of different income brackets — to live in the variety of townhouse and mid-rise housing types. This project, including numerous social programs for community revitalization, proposed both policy *and* design as the solution.

The vacuum of the inner city today clearly demands solutions with both political and spatial components. On the sociopolitical front, we must consider tools such as job training, social services, and education; incentive programs for home and business ownership; tax breaks and insurance programs to minimize risk-taking; and access to jobs outside the neighborhood, as well as job-generating businesses within the neighborhood. On the physical front, we must consider the building stock and its condition; the proximity of "problematic" activities such as garbage dumping and industry; the quality of housing, streets, parks, and infrastructure; and the need for parking and public transportation that are safe and widely available.

Much of the discussion of American social and economic structures in recent decades has focused on upward mobility as the ultimate goal. But physical mobility, increased interaction, and a newly accessible and versatile urban region are necessary and powerful tools for helping to fix the urgent problems of our city centers. In imagining the future of cities, it is time we recognize that the physical structure of our environment daily and fundamentally affects our experiences, and that the current levels of social malaise and economic dysfunction cannot persist within the inner city without seriously risking the health of our regions at large.

PART II

FACING
REALITY

CHAPTER 4

The Making
of Public Space

Defining the Public Realm

What makes a place feel public? In pre-automobile cities, public funds were spent to build post offices, courthouses, libraries, and places of governance and to maintain streets, piazzas, markets, and parks. These were the places for spon-

taneous interaction — a distinct realm, maintained by the public. In the nineteenth century, when entrepreneurs built the great gallerias of Italy, France, and Britain, no effort was spared to declare these places clearly in the public domain, an extension of the streets and piazzas of the city. Hence, Milan's Galleria Victor Emanuel of 1865 extended directly from one street to a public square

Galleria Victor Emanuel

through the city block, its interior floored with masonry, its glass roof flooding the space with light, and the shop facades defining the corridor as exterior in every respect: a smaller-scale commercial street connecting two larger public spaces.

Architects supported the architectural rules of this arrangement. A tradition of the "build-to" line — building right up to the sidewalk and joining each structure with its neighbors along the street — gave public outdoor space definition and cohesiveness, and these street facades were embellished and treated with decorum. The principal streets and squares were landscaped with grand trees and flowering gardens. The best sites were selected and designated for major buildings, such as Boston's public library facing Copley Place, or the New York Public Library on Bryant Park. Well-designed and well-maintained public parks — New York's Central Park, Montreal's Mount Royal Park, Boston's Emerald Necklace — stood as urban amenities for all. There was a consensus that the public domain was worthy of attention, a justifiable and appropriate investment of taxpayer dollars.

In the contemporary city, much of this has changed. As traditional streets of shops and local businesses were challenged and replaced by super-block commercial towers, parking, and interior-oriented malls, they deteriorated. Streets empty of pedestrians and of street-level entrances and windows became increasingly unsafe, and added to social polarization by making the public realm less attractive, comfortable, and commercially desirable. The growth of malls, country clubs, fitness centers, and atria of all kinds is a reaction to the absence of the old kind of public space, a retreat to a controlled and secured realm.

Today, primarily *private* funds are invested in constructing places for public congregation — even in cities that still possess the traditional street and square network. Public spaces of the nineteenth century, such as Quincy Market in Boston, were originally conceived as a continuous part of the city street network; yet in recent years even they have often been recycled as privately run, operated, and maintained enterprises. Far more common are new urban malls that differentiate themselves from the street with rarely more than a display window as a connection to their urban surroundings.

The Galleria Victor Emanuel served citizens who were not just shoppers, since it was the obvious and only connection between two places in the city. The contemporary urban mall, in contrast, is rarely designed for anyone but the pedestrian with the intention of spending money.

STAMFORD

I was invited to Stamford in 1972 by the F. D. Rich Company (which had been designated by the Stamford Redevelopment Authority to develop the downtown center) to discuss the city's growth patterns and planning. By the time of my arrival, a few high-rise office towers had been built in the downtown, including a headquarters for GTE and several smaller office buildings, and the urban renewal plan called for adding a mega-shopping center. With Stamford's growing population and business community, the mall appeared ripe for construction.

Asked to consider the design of this huge downtown project, I was concerned that the mall's massive infusion of retail space would be stiff competition for the traditional street-fronting downtown shops. And so I considered ways to establish as many visual and pedestrian links to the surrounding streets as possible. With a continuous flow of pedestrian traffic, I believed the shopping center could be designed actually to contribute to the city's existing commercial vitality. In the tradition of the day, however, the major focus was on building a "modern" mega-center for the area, and a large commercial developer was invited to complete it.

In 1982, the regional shopping center opened with 900,000 square feet of retail space. Trapped between parking structures on all four sides, the mall was effectively parachuted into the city, a hermetic world unto itself. As built, the mall was also sandwiched between several levels of parking above and below, lifting its ground floor two stories above the surrounding streets, atop a virtual cliff of parking structures. Instead of placing the shops at street level and connecting to existing streets and paths, the Stamford Mall designer chose to do the opposite: to raise the entire mall onto a podium above the city. And it has reinforced an urban pattern: the GTE Headquarters (built before the mall and poised over a three-story parking platform) and most other downtown corporate towers also present to the few remaining pedestrians a perpetual, mute wall along the street.

At street level, today's Stamford is both jarring and alienating. Leaving the multi-leveled, skylit mall, you are immediately deposited into the garage or onto streets that are themselves lined by the walls of four- and five-story parking structures serving both the mall and the many corporate headquarters. If you persevere down the empty avenues, following a sidewalk constantly interrupted by curb cuts into garages, trucking docks, and parking structures, you have only a disjointed street wall to guide you.

Nor does the mall attempt to relate to the corporate headquarters that have chosen Stamford as their place of business. The mall itself might have functioned physically like a street to provide access to the offices, hotels, apartments, and other structures that make up the downtown, offering goods and services demanded by large businesses. Yet the project was conceived from the beginning as disconnected — both programmatically and physically — from its environment inside and out. Pedestrians move among the various office complexes, the retail streets, and shopping center only with difficulty.

The central planning concept — to place a major shopping mall with ample parking in the heart of downtown, but close to the freeway — was in itself probably not a mistake. But, as in the case of Copley Place in Boston, the shopping center developer strongly supported a self-contained, introverted mall set apart from the life of the city. Instead of helping to develop vitality in the modern city center, the design of the mall precludes any active street life around it — and boldly and brashly destroys any remnants of past vitality as well.

While Stamford has all the ingredients necessary to be a vibrant center, including a museum (a branch of New York City's Whitney Museum) and a new local opera house, the individual components of a healthy urbanity have been located haphazardly. The urban design fails to synthesize pre- and post-automobile building types and to mesh the many mega-projects with a reasonable network of connections and circulation — in short, to create a whole city that is greater than its individual parts.

Privatizing the Public Realm

Shopping malls have become, as Witold Rybczynski describes, "for most Americans, the chief place to meet fellow citizens"[1] today. With public subsidies falling and operating costs rising, even traditionally independent civic institutions have begun to succumb to the power of private developers. On the condition that they are adjacent to, and entered from, the shopping mall, institutions such as Montreal's new Symphony Hall, as well as its hockey arena, are offered better sites than they can often afford independently. Although these public/private "marriages" constitute survival tactics for valuable cultural organizations, they also drastically impoverish the quality of the city out-of-doors as the private interior more and more comprehensively constitutes the focus of public life.

In dispersed areas, the effect of this privatization is even more extreme. Here, where no previously existing street or square must serve as a starting point, pure expediency governs the exterior impact of a new shopping or entertainment center. Once the basic operating requirements of ample parking, commercial square footage, and connections to the highway are fulfilled, private developers have little incentive to spend money and time on beautifying the site, landscaping the vast asphalt lots, mitigating the damage to adjacent residential neighborhoods and environments, or designing any aspect of the development's exterior but the signage. As privately owned shops depended on the public street a century ago, so, too, are today's mall and its stores dependent on, and nourished by, the highway. In turn, the highway and the mall together become the major components of the public realm.

Why have public spaces been preempted by privately constructed and controlled places? If suburban super-malls were the only manifestation of this new phenomenon, we might simply assume that private construction of the public realm has been the inadvertent result of a market trend: growing market demand for large-scale retail complexes generously served by parking, which are best accomplished by a single developer on cheap unbuilt land. But the continued growth of internalized malls and enclosed atria within the fabric of traditional downtowns, where land and parking costs are relatively high, suggests that there is more to this phenomenon than pure economic expediency.

Interior malls address the growing safety problems of cities (guns, drugs, desperate populations undermined by decades of poverty) for the very reason that they are private. At the Mall of America in suburban Minneapolis, 109 surveillance cameras proved insufficient, and the "security center" was compelled to add more.[2] Malls have become a way of turning over to the private domain the very real responsibility for policing, cleaning, and maintaining the public domain. Further, they provide urban mall developers with control over key factors in their investment: the merchants, the merchandise, and the clientele. "Control" and "security" are key words in a mall. Recent political battles have shown that developers will incorporate subway stations and other traditionally public services, for example, only when they judge that the "right" customers need access by public transportation, or when the city demands this "price" in exchange for a prime location.

Both in the suburban mall, isolated by its moat of parking lots, and in the urban mall, connected through its gateways to the truly public street, control and security are maintained through carefully crafted managerial procedures and interior design techniques. Physical design exerts control by the use of materials and techniques of circulation. With no doors and complete physical continuity with the surrounding streets and squares of the city, Milan's Galleria Victor Emanuel virtually becomes a component of the public realm. Most of our urban malls, on the contrary, explicitly differentiate themselves from the street with multiple sets of doors, stairs, escalators, and changes of level. The mall and atrium built by John Portman at Renaissance Center in Detroit (1979) is not unique in being almost completely undetectable from the street.[3] Whereas the Galleria Victor Emanuel emphasizes its publicness by the use of masonry floors, an open, ornate streetside facade, and plenty of daylighting inside, the contemporary mall usually broadcasts messages of exclusivity, interiority, and privacy in every detail. Floors are often polished marble, window framing is often chrome (like the lobbies of opulent office buildings), and daylight is typically kept to a minimum.

Ironically, it is in Las Vegas, in the most contrived of urban shopping centers, that we come full circle to the creation of a simulated exterior mall architecture, albeit in fiberglass and plaster-molded classical stage-set buildings. The developers, aiming to mimic a "Roman" street at Caesar's Palace, could not, however, go so far as allowing daylight. Instead, a painted sky with an artificial lighting system simulates daytime, dusk, or evening.

COLUMBUS CENTER

It was the strategies manifested in the Galleria Victor Emanuel that guided and inspired certain aspects of my design for the unbuilt Columbus Center in New York City, set at Columbus

Circle, the southwest corner of Central Park. A mixed-use, three-million-square-foot building, which included theaters, cinema complexes, two subway stations, and commercial, office, hotel, and residential space — the project was a microcosm of a city. And the central issue in my mind was how to relate those activities that were obviously private — the offices, hotel rooms, and residences — with those meant for the public at large.

Columbus Center in New York

My strategy was to design the public facilities as true extensions of the street, Columbus Circle, Central Park, and the two subway stations. Connecting 60th and 58th streets north–south around the circle, a long, curving, five-story-high daylit public gallery forms a main civic entrance facing Central Park South, the major east–west public thoroughfare. Doors are eliminated; stores are entered directly from both the outdoor street and the indoor gallery; and shops at both subway and street levels are clad in stone such as we see on the surrounding streets. From the gallery floor, a glass-roofed public garden can be seen two floors above, which serves as a forecourt for restaurants and a twelve-screen movie theater.

These ideas provoked a lot of discussion among the developer's team, as many argued for establishing an atmosphere of exclusivity to attract wealthier shoppers (and deter others), rather than serving the urban mix of the city. In this spirit, they preferred adding doors and interior design finishes to

Street facade of Columbus Center Galleria

the Gallery, and playing down as much as possible its connection to the two subway stations — a potential source of pedestrian traffic, but not of the "right" kind.

Such debates demonstrate the risk of entrusting our public spaces entirely to the good graces of the private sector — whose incentive, of course, is to achieve maximum value on any investment. The natural extension of this process of pure profit-oriented decision-making and little public involvement presents a profoundly disturbing view of the future city: that of a vast no-man's-land merely connecting a series of privately controlled oases.

Beyond the Shopping Mall

As long as we desire places to congregate, our cities will, one way or another, continue to represent an assemblage of publicly and privately controlled spaces. Although private malls and commercial atria, as they are often built today, present serious challenges to safeguarding an outdoor, pluralistic public realm, their success is also provocative.

This success, at the very least, is a vote of confidence in the ability of the private sector to construct and maintain public spaces more effectively than municipalities. Less willing to pay taxes for public amenities, today's public, apparently, will pay higher retail and entertainment prices to support their provision by private developers. Although there is little evidence

Interior of Galleria

that such endeavors are more effectively, more efficiently, or more economically handled by the private sector than by public agencies, it is clear that certain *types* of experiences currently offered by malls should be included in any type of future public space.

Yet, as we have seen, with its policies of exclusion and control emphasizing revenue, the modern mall is a poor replacement for the public domain. Therefore, we must go beyond the mall to invent a new breed of place, an "interactive center," which, whether in public or private hands, lives up to its role as a major component of the urban public realm.

What kind of place will this be? At the minimum, it must:

- connect different parts of the city, instead of establishing a district unto itself.
- integrate uses that are truly public by definition, such as courthouses, post offices, libraries, welfare offices, day-care, schools, and community centers.
- extend the public streets and spaces of the city, connecting to public transportation, to parking specifically for the center, and to general city parking.
- relate existing urban institutions in the city to the pedestrian circulation system throughout the center.
- relate interior space to existing outdoor parks, gardens, and playgrounds.
- present exterior architectural facades that form a continuum with buildings surrounding the center.
- avoid doors wherever possible and use modern technology, such as air curtains, to control climate.
- avoid interior-type finishes and use such exterior-type materials as masonry and other hard maintainable surfaces for floors.
- accommodate the changing seasons by opening to the outdoors and allowing fresh air.
- be richly endowed with daylight.

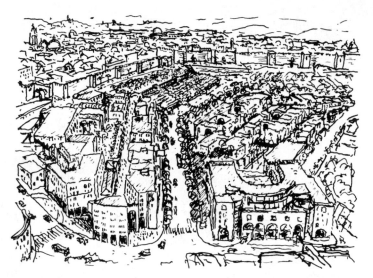

Aerial view of Mamilla Center looking toward the Old City, Jerusalem

MAMILLA

It is not often today that an entirely new center is built in the heart of an existing city, particularly one that is more than three thousand years old. Indeed, those examples that come to mind have not stood time's tests very convincingly. Urban renewal efforts such as Boston's government center, or shopping centers like the Prudential Center at the edge of Boston's Back Bay, today create such empty and unfriendly plazas that they make urban public space appear remarkably undesirable.

It was in this context that I faced with great trepidation the planning of Mamilla, a mixed-use center in the heart of Jerusalem, adjacent to Jaffa Gate, the Citadel, and the ancient city walls, and connecting the Old City with the New, the Israeli with Arab sectors. The rebuilding of Mamilla was not so much the result of an urban renewal decision, but of wars. A no-man's-land for nineteen years, the border between two divided cities, the district had deteriorated and been partially destroyed in battles. It was slated for rebuilding in 1972 after the city was unified in 1967.

Mindful of the pitfalls of downtown interventions elsewhere, could I do better? Could I provide parking without creating walls of parking garages along urban streets? Could I organize the lively bazaars of the Old City to form a continuum with other shopping streets in the district? Could I create a new center that meshed with the city around its entire perimeter? Could I, as the architect, guarantee a truly public character in Mamilla's streets and piazzas, and avoid the privatized ambiance of so many urban malls?

The answer lay in imbuing familiar forms with new meanings to meet Jerusalem's particular conditions. Thus, the pedestrian street closed down to traffic, so successfully introduced in cities like Copenhagen and Stuttgart, becomes the basis for Mamilla's "Cardo." Adopting the alignment of the historic Mamilla Street, it sets out from the connecting street system of Jerusalem and runs a quarter of a mile to the historic Jaffa Gate. In recognition of Jerusalem's unique climate, I opened the street to the sky, but provided it with a continuous, sheltered arcade for protection from the rain and sun. Its width is generous — thirty feet — and it breaks into open piazzas overlooking the historic valleys. Finally, the street is lined by buildings with facades of varying heights, with offices, hotels, and apartments above.

Like urban centers elsewhere, Mamilla encompasses a mix of uses, but even the commercial structures facing the pedestrian street never present their backs to the city. On the contrary, apartments and offices are accessed from the surrounding streets. Parking is never visible. The two thousand parking spaces and major bus terminal in Mamilla tuck under

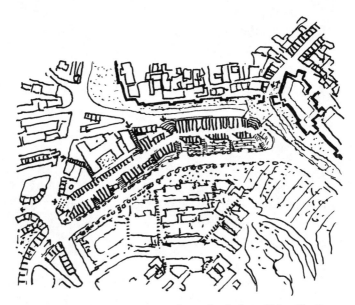

Street-level plan of Mamilla Center

Mamilla Street, fitted carefully into the topography so that all exterior walls become carefully planted terraced parks, connecting the historic valley and national park with the pedestrian streets above. When completed in 1999, Mamilla will seem to have been woven into the historic fabric of Jerusalem.

I considered this as a project of invisible mending, in the sense that each strand of fabric — each alley, each street, each mass of existing building — finds a continuity and counterpoint in the project that has been constructed in its midst.

Public/Private Domain

It is clear that many of the environmental qualities we would desire for a public place contradict the values of most current mall developers, whose interests bear more resemblance to those of a casino developer than those of an urban designer entrusted with the public domain. For as we have seen, it is supposed that daylight interferes with "commercial drama" inside; continuity with the surrounding city invites people not intending to spend money; and investment in any feature that does not directly support the exchange of money challenges basic cost–return formulas for a profit-making commercial development. The fundamental question — why should a private developer do anything to limit independent control over a large investment? — must receive the fundamental answer: because as a society, we acknowledge that private developers are now constructing *our* public domain. And therefore, they should be subject to public-minded planning and zoning.

As we acknowledge the central role of these public places in our social life, public life, and urban environment, we must acknowledge that even privately owned urban and suburban malls are already dependent on public investment. They depend on street access, on highways, and on heavy public investment in infrastructure. In urban malls, this dependence often extends to public subsidies for parking structures, atria, and interior landscaping. Horton Plaza in San Diego, Harborplace in Baltimore, and Peachtree Plaza in Atlanta were all heavily subsidized by public funds. Do they not automatically owe the public certain minimum standards of amenity and access?

Further, if the mall preempts the street, must it not, in any case, preserve the legal rights, public character, and accessibility of the public street of old? Can a U.S. citizen, for example, distribute leaflets for political causes, or address mall shoppers under the rights of the First Amendment? Such rights have been reaffirmed in airports, libraries, and other facilities constructed with public funds, but only recently, in very limited fashion, in privately owned malls.

Even in a political climate generally suspicious of regulations, we have in recent years, in cities all over the world, devised complex regulatory devices to meet certain goals of urban planning policy. We mandate parking square footages, building densities and uses, and particularly in historic districts, we establish aesthetic standards.

Yet to date, such regulations have completely avoided the public issues of privately owned urban spaces. And although cities like Toronto, Vancouver, New York during the Lindsay administration, and, from time to time, Boston under the Boston Redevelopment Authority, have attempted to contribute to the design of private malls, time and time again, as Toronto's Eaton Centre and Boston's Copley Place demonstrate, these intentions are overwhelmed by the developers' enormous financial leverage.

Therefore, facing the future of the regional city with open eyes, a profound question necessarily arises: if private commercial realms constitute the new public domain, and as writer David Guterson has put it, "exploit our acquisitive instincts without honoring our communal requirements,"[4] then how will the public realm be included (if at all) in the city of the future?

CHAPTER 5
Working in the City

The high-rise tower is the hallmark of the late twentieth-century city. Practically and symbolically, the skyscraper is the dominant building type, its impact affecting every facet of urban life, its scale affecting the very form of the city. Towers have resolved certain of society's needs for density and concentration, and have opened up new ways of experiencing space. But their dominance does not mean that we, as designers or as users of these super-scale structures, have succeeded in resolving the many environmental and urbanistic issues they pose. We have yet to use high-rise towers as an effective urban building block. We have yet to make them uplifting places to live or work. We have become dependent upon high-rise buldings, but we have also been compromised by them. How have these unwieldy, yet often breathtakingly elegant, buildings come to shape our urban lives so dramatically?

The City Grows Up
In the beginning there was the village, and then the city, the height of their buildings dictated by the distances people could climb — four, or perhaps five, stories. Based on the scale and size of these walk-up buildings, the organization of the city's streets and public spaces developed over centuries, and evolved in relationship to the transportation systems, building materials, and

technology of the times. This basic scale of cities, for centuries closely related to human measure, was shattered (or liberated, depending on your view) by the invention of concrete frame structures, the Otis elevator, and Bessemer steel. This did not occur, of course, by chance, but in direct response to the quickening pace of commerce and congestion in the nineteenth-century city — a result of opportunity and necessity combined. Urban buildings soon soared in height, first in Chicago and New York, and quickly thereafter in cities all over the world.

Tall-building design pioneers struggled with the proportions and organization of this new breed of architecture. In their early phases, in the 1870s and for several subsequent decades, the floor plates of most towers remained relatively small, limited by their inherited lot sizes and by the need, before air-conditioning systems, to provide most interior spaces with exposure to the building's perimeter. Because they were built in the place of low-rise commercial buildings, their plans were similar — modified only to accommodate an enlarged core of elevator banks and fire stairs. Most floors consisted of a sequence of rooms, each with a window, served by a tight central core.

In style, early tower designs ranged from neoclassical and Gothic to more original variations by Louis Sullivan and others, but most were composed of a base, middle, and top section considered as discrete and constituent parts of the whole. The base often contained shops, and an effort was made to defer to the life of the street. These designers were urbanists at heart, preoccupied with the scale of buildings as they were perceived by the pedestrian, and with the manner in which each one, side by side with its neighbor, contributed to forming the continuous public space of the street.

By the time of the 1922 competition to design the Chicago Tribune Building, however, a clear theoretical and stylistic divide had developed among designers over the appropriate expression of tall buildings. Generally speaking, the traditionalists attempted to address the building's unprecedented scale by manipulating its massing to differentiate the public, private, commercial, or residential components, individuating windows and entrances, and creating compositions with a variety of traditionally crafted masonry details. The modernists united all components of the building into a simple extruded object with a thin, repetitive — and less costly — outer skin. This "winning" modernist ideology made a virtue of what was essentially an architecture of economic expediency.

The impact of tall buildings on the city was profound. And as the canyon syndrome set in — high-rise buildings cutting off sun and light from each other and from the street — the idea emerged that zoning ordinances could help moderate the negative impact of these proliferating skyscrapers on the city as a whole. As early as 1916, provoked by the sheer massiveness of the forty-two-story Equitable Building, New York City passed its first zoning ordinance to prohibit towers that presented continuous walls from base to top and blocked daylight entirely from the public realm below. Known as the "setback law," the ordinance related the height of the building wall to the width of the street that it bordered, and specified different levels at which the building be "set back" from the street as it extended upward into the air. Each neighborhood received guidelines specific to the particular character of its streets.[1]

Keeping the streets and sidewalks more open to light, sun, and sky, the progressive setback had a decisive effect both outside and inside the mass of the tower. Stepping back from the street as they rose, a new generation of ziggurat-like towers took their places along New York's streets, and, like sparks of energy, helped to generate a more intricate, more dynamic urban skyline. Transforming the interior spaces of towers as well, the jagged profile created a series of terraces and roof gardens — outdoor spaces for both office and residential uses.

At Rockefeller Center (1931–39) in New York City, an awareness of the partnership between the shape of the tower and of the space around it developed even further. Here, the building–street relationship was delicately and masterfully studied. Combining different heights of towers and lower buildings within one city block moderated the impact of the tower at ground level and allowed for pedestrian alleys and piazzas in the block's interior. With rows of stores and comfortable outdoor public spaces, these secondary pedestrian precincts became natural extensions of the major city streets, and extended the domain of the public realm into the domain of the building. Driven by zoning laws, the skyscrapers of an era thus were shaped to preserve and enhance the urban experience at street level.

Beginning in the 1950s, the emphasis in tower design became more closely focused on perceiving the building as an independent entity in the city, rather than as part of a street wall that shaped public spaces. Mies van der Rohe, in his early designs, and later the firm Skidmore Owings and Merrill and other firms evolved for the office building an entirely new role in the urban design of the city — that of a sculptural object. Using the ground plane as a kind of stage for a unique event, the tower was conceived as singular, its simple shape and undifferentiated skin cut off, seemingly arbitrarily, where it hit the ground and reached the sky.

As the white-collar workforce expanded exponentially and building technology evolved, with faster elevators and air-conditioning allowing large, artificially ventilated interiors — corporations generally responded with economic expediency.

Its broad, repetitive floor plates, simplified massing, and standardized surface treatments made the Miesian vision of a minimalist extruded tower a convenient model. Increasingly vast, windowless work areas became an accepted answer to the need for more space, with air-conditioning commonly replacing windows that open and other methods of natural ventilation. To serve greater areas, elevator cores got fatter; to accommodate more people and services, the girth of tall buildings continued to grow.

By 1961, the setback law in New York City had been entirely dismantled as ever larger envelopes of space presented ever greater challenges to the traditional urban fabric. The simpler floor–area ratio ordinance enacted in its place (in which the total volume of the tower is regulated according to its lot size) allowed bonus heights for outdoor public areas — and the abstract and simple towers, of which Mies's 1958 Seagram Building was the paradigm, were thus encouraged by policy to break away from the street edge, "free," so to speak, in an open space referred to as a "plaza."

By today's standards of office tower behemoths, the original modern prototypes like Mies's Seagram Building or Gordon Bunshaft's Lever House are slender and delicate. But within a decade of the Seagram Building, dozens of buildings in New York (and many other cities) had grown to take whole blocks for their sites, with plazas — vast, sheer, and empty — encouraged by subsidies of public funding and bonus zoning. Disrupting the continuity and containment that had existed for the pedestrian in the historic city street, in effect, the plaza represented a total denial of the tradition of urban space. And perceived from the street or plaza, each modern tower was exaggerated in size and scale as pedestrians stood back to see these giant buildings crashing — all fifty floors — into the ground plane.

In the newer automobile cities, particularly during the 1970s and 1980s, towers ballooned in scale in an even more extreme fashion. Unlike San Francisco, Chicago, New York, Philadelphia, and Boston, cities such as Dallas, Houston, Denver, and São Paulo were less constrained by historic street and parcelization patterns. Moreover, while in Chicago and New York most office workers continued to come to work by foot or by some form of mass transportation, practically all office workers in the newer cities arrived by car. Parking issues in these cities were urgent. With block sizes often larger than those in traditional urban centers, towers were built to occupy whole city blocks at minimum, with many levels below grade for parking. Roofs of the underground garages became plazas, and where conditions permitted, cheaper above-ground garages appeared as low and clunky appendages to office towers. Beyond the old downtown, practically every tower today is accompanied by its large five-story cousin: the parking structure.

By the 1980s, having dominated the downtowns for almost thirty years (and even spread into the periphery of most cities), modernist towers began to provoke wrath on the part of the public, and a second cycle of compositional invention on the part of architects. The repetitive monotony of scale, envelope, and massing, the expanses of undifferentiated walls slicing off suddenly at the sky, the mammoth and absolute presence of these towers seemed to have run their course as an urban aesthetic. Drawing upon techniques similar, in some ways, to those explored in the earliest high-rise towers, designers once again attempted to break down scale and create unique identity in the skyline. Again seeking to delineate bases, tops, and setbacks, these designers employed varied materials that, without resorting to the earlier use of costly individually crafted cut stone or cast terracotta, created curtain walls of different kinds of glass, metal,

precast concrete, and thinly cut textured and colored stone —
but continued to view their towers as singular objects in the
urban landscape.

Cities of Towers

High-rise urbanism, as we have seen both in theory and in practice, was born with fundamental contradictions: unresolved
tensions between viewing towers as intrinsic parts of a dense
downtown and treating them as self-sufficient elements in the
environment. Not surprisingly, the result of this confusion is a
desultory and compromised high-rise city.

According to Le Corbusier, the tall building demanded an
enormous grid — not 400 feet by 225 feet as on the east side
of midtown Manhattan, for example, but instead, a super-grid
of 2,000 or 3,000 feet across, as if the goal of the tower as a form
were to allow the space of the surrounding city to become
mostly park. Thus, the most compelling image of modernist
urbanism fundamentally negated the tower's historic rationale
and the original impetus of urbanism, which was to gain the
economic benefits of bringing a large number of people or
businesses as close together as possible — close to transit, close
to services, and close to each other.

In practice, the new skyscraper was simply imposed on an
old urban structure, on street scales and lot sizes that significantly predated buildings whose shadows extended hundreds
of feet, whose impact on wind and air circulation was profound,
and whose tops towered over the sidewalks below. Further, in
most of North America and in newer cities around the world,
that original urban structure was an "undifferentiated"[2] grid,
which meant that no hierarchy created by principal routes,
unusual natural features, or an ordered pattern of civic buildings and spaces acted to guide the placement of towers in the

city as a whole. Commercial skyscrapers thus sprouted haphazardly to produce our current disordered matrices.

Recently, courthouses, museums, concert halls, performing arts centers, libraries, and institutions of governance have begun to seek financing by selling to developers their "air rights" and buildable areas allowed by zoning. Forced to "hitch a ride" with commercial mega-structures, civic and cultural institutions must now relegate the choice of their sites to secondary importance, and their own visibility and presence in the city has, in many cases, been drastically diminished as a result. Not the product of grand plans, but of circumstance and pragmatism, the configuration of the city of towers we see today has emerged, therefore, almost accidentally.

The Workspace of Towers

Towers have become the most common solution to providing urban corporations and institutions with workspace, but they have also become increasingly unpleasant to the people who spend much of their lives inside them. Typically designed to satisfy considerations of the building's facade, the interiors of towers are rarely determined by consideration for their inhabitants or the types of spaces they provide. In service only of the exterior design, large expanses of glass or small punched windows are designed abstractly, regardless of whether a wall faces north or south, whether it might screen the horizontal setting sun or admit diffuse light. No matter what the climate, windows rarely open, trapping stale recirculated air inside. Finally, acting as compositional devices (and sometimes acting to control the energy costs of poorly designed exterior envelopes), colored, reflective, or tinted glasses are used without concern for employees, who now see the world through colored glass (usually murky brown or green) on sunny and cloudy days, daytime and nighttime, eight hours each day through the course of every working year.

To accommodate the growing number of people they are designed to hold, commercial floor plates have grown increasingly large and increasingly crowded. With floor areas ten to fifteen times larger than the early towers, typical contemporary office buildings maintain stacks of twenty, thirty, or even forty elevators with restrooms and mechanical spaces at their core — a layer of space thirty to sixty feet deep with an outer rim of windows wrapping the perimeter. The organization is familiar: a few managers and other senior executives are given offices with windows, but daylight remains scarce in the greater portion of these workspaces. A larger number of mid-level managers are given private, but interior, offices. A maze of windowless meeting rooms and service areas borders the elevators, and the majority of the workforce is relegated to "open," subdivided workspace, defined by low partitions and almost always without any natural light at all. The floors are stacked, completely uniform in their eight-and-a-half or nine-foot heights, and lit by a grid of fluorescent fixtures. It is often hard to believe that our workplaces, described by writer Douglas Coupland as "veal-fattening pens,"[3] were designed specifically for us to work in.

Working with the Workplace

The quality of life within towers is a low (indeed, often absent) priority among designers and the public alike. It has not been a central theme in the academic discourse, and the many books published about towers focus almost exclusively on the tower as a decorative or structural object. Many of the developments of postmodernism, such as using reflective glass and highly sophisticated curtain walls, were aimed at giving total interior flexibility, allowing a design to be adaptable to virtually any orientation or geography from Minneapolis and Chicago to Riyadh and Singapore. None has had anything to do with the quality of the working environment or the spatial experience within.

Over the last decade some efforts to focus on "human" concerns, such as qualities of light and interior space, have led to more organic and responsive exterior skins and daylighting devices such as new types of light shafts and atria. In these respects, Norman Foster's Hong Kong and Shanghai Banking Corporation Headquarters and his Frankfurt Commerzbank Headquarters reveal the potential for a future "neo-humanism" in tower design. To achieve significant change, however, our preoccupations in the design of the tall office building must shift from superficial composition, totally independent of the life within the structure, to the quality of its interior space and the way in which it relates to the city.

Instituting even the most minimal environmental standards could completely transform the design of office towers. We know that exposure to the exterior is essential to mental and psychological well-being, essential to preventing fatigue. The ability to focus visually on short and long distances and the relief of knowing whether it is day or night, rainy or sunny, affect everyone's daily experience. In 1901, the New York Tenement House Law required that all habitable rooms in residential buildings receive daylight. Imagine requiring today that no one spend a working day, the majority of daytime hours, without the benefit of natural light. We could regulate and vary ceiling heights according to the type of activity and number of people each space contains. We could, for example, accept low spaces for small private offices, but in large spaces that accommodate fifty or a hundred people, require extra height proportionate to the size of the room.

But the workday is not restricted to a workstation, and the

office tower must include a variety of spaces for solitary work and for collaborative work; for video interaction and for personal exchange; for working as well as for socializing. There must be places for meeting, eating, daycare, and recreation, areas that foster interaction during breaks, at lunch, and after work. Confronting these issues in design will lead inevitably to manipulating the building's massing to increase daylight, diversifying the heights of interior spaces and the window treatment according to solar exposure, and introducing community amenities like garden lounges and social spaces within the building, each uniquely endowed. The repetitive stacking of enormous floor plates must give way to a three-dimensionally more intricate concept of space.

The Dutch architect, Herman Hertzberger, in his seminal project near Amsterdam for the insurance company Centraal Beheer (1968–72), demonstrated how private work areas, daylight, lounges for coffee and discussions, even gardens, can be three-dimensionally configured to create a stimulating workplace. Why should we not work in places that can be shaped uniquely: protective and expressive of the individual, but also part of a larger, collective space? Will individuals eventually recognize the cost of submitting to the expedient "mega-space" now provided for them? Will they wonder whether closed and shut rooms and enormous recurring floor plates with minimal potential for vertical spatial connections, daylight, or contact with the outdoors constitute desirable workspaces? Ultimately, those who inhabit commercial skyscrapers must face a fundamental question of privacy versus community.

A long-standing premise of the clients, architects, developers, and inhabitants of tall office buildings is that all can be achieved by partitioning a vast, low, and scaleless sandwich of a space. To recognize, instead, the *diversity* that is possible inside the space of a tower will constitute the difference between a sense of well-being and oppressiveness, generosity and deprivation. We just might find that freeing the interior office landscape from perpetual repetition will, in turn, free the office tower from its uniform curtain-walled envelope entirely.

Envisioning a High-Rise Urbanism

The issue of the tower in the city requires a concept of urbanity specifically constituted for towers and conceived to create public and private places both within and between them. In this context, the undifferentiated grid clearly never was the optimal answer. To integrate towers effectively into the city, we must develop a new rationale to locate public structures and civic institutions in a meaningful way, envision a new kind of place in which the tower is *the* building block — and drastically reexamine the design of towers themselves.

As towers became the dominant urban building type, they created severe scale problems next to lower buildings, disrupted streets that had worked well as public spaces, caused shadows and wind drafts randomly, and often compounded these problems by taking up large volumes of space above or below ground for parking. Today's city streets strain under decades' accumulation of these pressures. And beyond the limits of downtown, any connective urban fabric is highly dysfunctional or nonexistent. Betraying a certain resignation, theoretical and actual proposals for rethinking the effective use of towers to form a collective — a district, part of a city, or entire city — have been few.

Today, tall buildings in the regional city appear in two general configurations. Still dominant are towers packed densely throughout the grid of the traditional center and along preserved open spaces to form an edge. In contrast is the loose, almost random, grouping of towers along freeways. If you fly over Toronto, Vancouver, Houston, or the outskirts of Chicago, you see within an area of twenty-five square miles two to three dozen "eruptions" of tall buildings, scarcely related to the road, interspersed with low-density suburban development, in no discernible pattern.

Yet we know the life and quality of an urban community is greatly affected by the configuration of tall buildings. Working adjacent to the Boston Common is fundamentally different from working at an isolated site on the rim of the regional city. As we think about future urban developments and the quality of urban life, it becomes essential to consider the design of towers in relation to the city as a whole and the ways in which they might relate to one another on the ground and in the air. Towers depend on proximity to parking and road access, public transportation, and a wealth of services and amenities needed by those who populate them; inherently, they are not self-sufficient. Inventing a new kind of tower in the city immediately concerns inventing a new kind of city street — the glue that binds single buildings into cities.

Today, we must recognize the ground from which the tower rises, and discover and invent a new urban base to receive, support, and connect the people and the buildings. And when we do, the urban tower will be vibrant with life — more than today's cold and glinting obelisk, draped in masonry and glass, and buzzing exhaustively in monotone.

CHAPTER 6

Living in the City

From the detached house through the attached row house, townhouse, crescent, or atrium house to the urban tenement, the apartment block, and finally (with the advent of elevators) the high-rise tower, habitation in the city has responded to increasing demands for concentration. As the forms of our public realm and places of work have changed along with forms of technology and society — so too has evolved the third major element of all cities: the place of residence.

Although relatively recent in historical terms, the high-rise apartment structure has become the almost universal response to housing in cities today. To be sure, vast amounts of relatively low-rise housing continue to be built in expanded regional cities — from single-family tract homes in North America to densely packed *favelas* and *barrios* in the Third World. But increasingly, in the centers and at the perimeters of cities, for the poor, middle-income, and affluent, the high-rise, elevator-dependent apartment building emerges worldwide as the predominant urban home.

Mass Housing
Two economically diverse markets have influenced both the location and the design of residential towers: mass public housing and market-sensitive, "luxury" housing. The images for mass

public housing were supplied in the 1920s and 1930s from the realm of architectural theory: the annals of CIAM; Le Corbusier's visions of a *Ville Radieuse* and a *Cité de Trois Milles* (1922); Ludwig Hilberseimer's *Hochhausstadt* project (1924); and other grand urban schemes. To the designers of such visions, an urban dweller's wish for a unique identity, for differentiation, and, hence, variety in housing was antiquated: an historic impediment to be transcended. Ostensibly, the "modern" person would overcome bourgeois inclinations of the nineteenth century in pursuit of a broader social purpose. Government agencies would dispense equal accommodations to each inhabitant of a town, district, or entire city, and the resulting uniformity would constitute social justice.

Housing, therefore, became primarily a tool for social change, and not a means of satisfying the (assumedly corrupt) demands of popular taste. To early modern architects, acting in

Perspective of Hochhausstadt *project by Hilberseimer*

the sequestered realm of theory, uniform repetition in the built environment became an attractive idea — even an ideal. "Repetition," wrote Hilberseimer in 1927, "is no longer regarded as something to be avoided . . . for identical needs, identical buildings."[1] According to architect and member of CIAM Bruno Taut, "the first requirement in every building is the achievement of the greatest possible utility."[2]

Such theorizing conveniently dovetailed with objective conditions: an emerging urban middle class needed to be housed rapidly and efficiently. Producing large numbers of apartments for millions of families required cheap, uncomplicated construction, but it was almost inadvertent that these tracts of modernist high-rise buildings became the symbol and expression of socialist ideology. With pressures from immigration, post-war and post-colonial rebuilding, and a population flow into cities, many countries were charging their housing authorities with the construction of whole "neighborhoods," all at one time, on large tracts of land, with the greatest economy possible.

Because the construction of most of this "social housing" (as the Europeans called it) operated outside the forces of the market, site selection and design decisions alike were influenced by operational expediency. To achieve density, towers were constructed in the repetitive forms of tall, columnar buildings, or long, wall-like "slab" buildings, both forms that maximized the number of individual dwellings, while minimizing the number of expensive service cores. Out of concern for speed and economy, mixing low-rise, mid-rise, and high-rise building types was deemed excessively complicated: the number of building configurations was minimized to two or three per development. And for budgetary and administrative reasons, the same architectural plans were used again and again. Thus emerged the standard plan of thousands of housing developments in every

European city after the war, in Singapore and Hong Kong, in Taipei, Beijing, São Paulo and Mexico, in Caracas and Bombay, and in the United States in the 1950s and 1960s: a series, sometimes stacked across the site, of slab buildings intermingled with vertical towers.

The sites for such projects were either already vacant land at the edges of expanding cities, or, more often, specific areas of the city created by clearing existing neighborhoods entirely. In both cases, with the traditional street pattern erased (as in Boston's West End and Cathedral Housing), or where a street system had never existed (Co-op City in the Bronx), the land surrounding the towers was intended as park space; in practice, much of this land became parking lots, as in New York's Peter Cooper and Stuyvesant Town, Boston's Cathedral Housing, and Montreal's Jeanne Manse. Further, public housing has rarely exploited even an adjacent natural amenity. You would never know from looking at its site plan, for example, that Stuyvesant Town borders the East River; but in this, it is similar to developments built by the public sector all over the world.

Housing on the Edge
The relentless character of post-war urban "social" housing contrasts vividly with the less regimented, more humane, and generally more appealing places to live in the city for those with a choice. Because private land purchases tend to be relatively small, as a rule, a single developer builds only one or two buildings at a time. Different architects designing different building forms with different materials have produced urban neighborhoods with natural variety. Design features ranging from the trivial (posh lobbies with fancy materials and uniformed doormen) to the significant (balconies and terraces, penthouses and rooftop units, bay windows and more generous fenestration,

and shorter, ventilated corridors) create a sense of individual address and identity to attract potential residents.

With developers seeking the most attractive sites for housing for the affluent, apartment buildings gravitated from the beginning toward the choice locations in the city, locations with natural amenities: distant views, the water's edge, adjacency to great parks and open spaces. This linear clustering of high-rise towers produced a new urban pattern — housing on the edge. Such private development occurred first along dramatic open spaces, such as Chicago's Lake Shore Drive and Manhattan's East River, Hudson River shore, and Central Park, and in most seashore and harbor cities along the coast. But as urban edges were built up, they created a corollary problem. They formed walls against the city behind them.

In almost every city today, apartments and hotels are packed along particular alignments. In Boston, prime housing lines the Public Garden and the Common; in Miami and Tel Aviv, hotels and apartments cluster, wall-like, by the shore; in Rio, the Copacabana's apartment blocks and hotels curve, massive and solid, to line the beach. Development along rivers, large parks, and permanent undeveloped land manifests the widespread desire for openness within cities, but typically, the built result effectively denies this valued feature to all but the relatively few who can afford to "buy" it. Thus, for the privileged who live along Lake Shore Drive there is the pleasure of Lake Michigan, but for those behind, a substantial wall against the lake.

This effect is not new; city planners have long struggled to find ways of keeping urban edges visibly and physically accessible to the population at large. When urban buildings were restricted to the height people could climb ("walk-up" buildings, as in Rome along the Tiber or Paris along the Seine), the challenges related to circulation: moving pedestrians and vehicles both along and toward the desirable edge. But the advent of urban towers (which was recent in terms of urban history) complicated the problem further: because of their height and girth, skyscrapers and superblocks shut out views and access to desirable edges much more completely than buildings ever had before.

The traditional technique for arranging tall buildings with respect to an edge has been to preserve a "view corridor" — an open vista down the length of streets from the interior toward the edge. For those moving along street level, these slices of light and space quite effectively open views, but in between these "corridors," long, continuous walls of buildings block the edge.

SIMPANG

Since the founding of the state of Singapore, the government has made a priority of providing housing for its growing population. As historic Singapore became fully built, the government developed a national plan to create a series of new towns around the island, linked by a system of highways and mass transit. In the past fifteen years, several new towns have been built according to the official formula: high-rise slab buildings organized around large courtyards. Only schools and community shopping are accommodated in low buildings, and as these towns each house more than 100,000 people, the result is an extensive area of high-rise towers of similar height. Visiting a new town, you ride the elevator to the top of a tower only to find that any distant view is reserved for those who live on the perimeter of the neighborhood. For most residents, looking out means staring into yet another apartment across a courtyard.

Early in the 1990s, with Singapore's standard of living and public expectations on the rise, this approach to housing

Typical new town Singapore, circa *1980s*

began to concern several planners at the Housing and Development Board. Because Singapore's land resources were severely restricted by the small area of the island city-state, all remained in agreement that high densities were required. But within the agency, a raging debate developed between those who felt the environment of new towns could be improved, and those convinced that the "formula" represented the optimal economic and design solution. In the context of this debate, I was invited in 1993 to develop alternative concepts for the Simpang New Town, to be built on the northern part of the island, facing the Strait of Johor, and looking toward Malaysia.

As we began to discuss the project, the housing board officials became greatly concerned that, working in my Boston office, my colleagues and I might ignore fundamental planning principles or living patterns particular to Singaporeans, and their senior architects and planners wanted to participate in our "charrette" — the intense, sustained work session that would characterize much of our two-month design effort. Thus, after a series of site visits and briefings, I returned to Boston with four Singaporean architects.

The site, almost square and facing the sea, was well served by Singapore's new subway system and ring highway. But the flat land extended deep inland, and in the official plan prepared for this site, most units blocked the light from one another; only those dwelling along the water's edge were offered the pleasure of an open vista. Therefore, when I began the design for Simpang New Town, I made it our objective to maximize living opportunities on the open edge — to create as many residences as possible that looked out to distant vistas — and to produce a new design at the same high density as the official plan.

We began the design exercise using high-rise towers as building blocks. Working with our large model of the site, however, it rapidly became apparent that our assumption, that only high-rise buildings could satisfy the required high densities, would prevent the kind of formal transformation we were looking for. As we explored the options, we combined low- and high-rise housing types to make the town plan much more diverse. The low-rise buildings, three and four stories high, would be planned and built "within the trees," surrounded by nature — with gardens, roof terraces, and small-scale parks. By creating large areas of low-rise, but high-density, cluster apartments, we were then able to arrange high-rise buildings in linear formations, with large open spaces between them.

As a civic focus for the town, we combined the schools, shopping areas, and other community amenities with playgrounds and parks to create a central, low-rise linear district along which high-rise structures could be concentrated. In this way, we were effectively creating new, "interior" built edges: inner lines of tall buildings with qualities of space, views, and light similar to those at the edges of the site.

But when we turned to the original, spectacular edge — the line of seashore with views toward Malaysia — the idea of concentrating high-rise buildings there seemed as aggressive as building a wall. As in so many coastal resorts where hotels and apartments crowd along the water, we would be forming a barrier that cut off many of the town's residents from a view of the sea. It was at this point that we began to develop a particular shape for those buildings along the coast: the form of a thirty-story wall pierced with fifteen- or twenty-story openings at regular intervals, almost like a monumental viaduct one could live in. The upper part of the buildings provided a great number of apartments with open views

Simpang New Town with spine of central park and community facilities

across the sea and city, while the lower levels formed giant windows from the street and lower buildings, providing the inland neighborhoods with views to the coast and allowing the sea breeze to sweep across the entire development.

The mix of low- and high-rise housing opened up new opportunities to create a dynamic building topography to replace the official uniform towers: a plan that recreated and expanded the quality of urban edges in built form. Terraced high-rise towers pierced by "urban windows," ridge-like, but permeable, followed the coastline. Within the site, these ridges recurred as series of apartment towers that acted like "internal edges" along the linear park and each edge of the site — like a series of steep and slender mountain ridges, pierced with open passes and separated by valleys of low-rise housing, community buildings, and parks. Thus, almost all the tall buildings in Simpang ended up in linear formations, with generous open spaces to their front and back.

"Urban windows," Simpang New Town

We returned to Singapore eight weeks later, the model shipped in sections to be assembled in the Housing Board's huge conference room. The official plan sat in model form on an enormous table next to ours, presenting a relentless and uninterrupted assemblage of tall buildings. Looking at it, the density was overwhelming. Our alternative concept, with its linear park and vast areas of low-rise buildings, created an openness that completely transformed the town's sense of space. There was a sense of disbelief as officials came into the room, convinced that we had changed the rules of the game, that we had reduced the density they had considered sacrosanct. And so, as ten young architects from the Housing Board's staff were called in, our tabulations of the density and number of housing units for our scheme were put away. Three days of analysis of each and every building, in minute detail, finally produced a new set of density calculations . . . and the numbers were identical.

Towers of Dwellings

The basic organization and architectural features of apartment towers have remained almost unchanged over the last forty years. Within an effectively static envelope, designers have produced different relationships between individual apartments; they have designated varying proportions of public and private spaces, and developed myriad improvements in building services. But the ubiquitous, artificially ventilated and lit corridor, buried between apartments on either side, remains a singularly unlikely place for sitting, talking, playing, or any kind of community interaction at all. The trip from outdoors — riding the elevator and traversing the stuffy corridor to an apartment — remains a major reason people have preferred low-rise housing. And while balconies, roof penthouses, and bay windows do create connections between the apartment within the block and the world of nature outside, these features pale in comparison to the amenities offered by alternative forms of habitation like single-family houses.

Consider the qualities of the single-family house that we have come to take for granted: privacy, multiple exterior exposures, private entry visible from the street, extensive and accessible outdoor space, garages and carports attached to the living space. We intuitively prefer rooms that look out in more than one direction; light streaming in from multiple directions is psychologically different from light entering only one of four walls. We experience this in the difference between a typical hotel room with windows facing a view or courtyard, and a corner suite with windows in two directions. Moreover, one of the most frustrating aspects of living in a high-rise building is its inaccessibility to the outdoors — its removal from the ground and fresh air, even the weather, not to mention the range of activities like sitting in a garden, reading, eating, or celebrating outdoors. These opportunities are all but absent from the typical high-rise residential tower.

HABITAT

Thirty years ago, such concerns generated my design of Habitat. I began with the assumption that we might design "houses" in the air, with open streets, clustered like a village but occurring in a city. If we could break loose from a simplistic envelope into a liberated three-dimensional matrix, we might be able to create the amenities of a house in the form of a high-rise residential tower. I was compelled by the desire to provide distant long views for each and every dwelling, and therefore was delighted to have a site that could be called "double-edged": a linear strip bordered

Habitat '67

by water and dramatic views out from either side.

Habitat emerged as a structure maximizing exposure, with each and every apartment looking out in three or four directions. To increase the number of walls from which the views could be seen, I folded and bent the perimeter of the building in intricate three-dimensional patterns. At the time, I did not realize I was pursuing an exercise in fractal geometry: beginning with a single vertical plane facing the view, and then breaking it up, undulating it, stepping it back — fractalizing it with a particular end in mind. I had not, of course, heard of Mandelbrot's term, "fractal," but I realized then the great potential of maximizing a built edge.

In studying the options for clustering the dwellings, I was troubled about the potential solid mass of the building as it lined the river. Accordingly, I organized the clusters of apartments with major gaps in between, opening dramatic views of the sky and the city — forming great holes in the otherwise massive wall of the building.

Substituting exterior walkways for interior corridors, shaping the building's mass to create roof gardens, multiple exposures, acoustic privacy, and articulating the scale of individual dwellings allowed Habitat to combine some of the amenities of single-family housing with the unique opportunities of a high-rise building. The result evoked a

Cross-section through Habitat houses, roof gardens, and pedestrian streets

village, hill town, or vertical housing cluster, rather than an impersonal behemoth, to which the existence and scale of an individual dwelling is subordinated behind a uniform skin of relentless, identical windows. As the Habitat complex was built and inhabited, a change in perception immediately occurred on the part of its residents: corridor became street, apartment became house, and balcony became garden. The pleasures of living with privacy were added to the benefits of living in close community.

The tremendous gap between the experience of living in a house versus a high-rise apartment tower has played a large part in fueling our decades-long exodus from the realm of downtown. If we are to confront the problem of our cities realistically, the tall building must be reevaluated for the type of residential space it provides, as well as for its role in urban design. Inherent in this question are many issues: for example, how the building and the individual apartment are entered, as well as the spatial qualities of the dwelling itself — the number of exposures, visual and acoustic privacy, the availability of outdoor space contiguous to the dwelling. These matters are subtle, but they are critical. They will make the difference between urban variety that satisfies the differing needs of families and individuals, and cookie-cutter uniformity; between a place in unison with nature, and one detached and cut off from it; and ultimately, between community and isolation.

The design of post–Second World War era urban housing reveals a significant gap between the popular tastes, desires, and aspirations expressed in market-rate housing, and those of the architectural avant-garde, more directly embodied in social housing. At the time, while private developers were responding to the taste of the market with the stylistically eclectic and decorated facades we see in the affluent neighborhoods of New York or Chicago, the leading architects were designing considerable numbers of uniform and stylistically austere modernist public housing projects and prototypes. Ridiculed and highlighted in Tom Wolfe's *From Bauhaus to Our House* (1981), this conflict between public taste and the values of the design profession has only deepened in recent decades, with the truly regrettable consequence — for the public as well as the architectural profession — of diminishing society's faith in the role of the architect, and the architect's ability (and inclination) to contribute to the public built environment.

But no one — neither from the public at large nor even the affluent consumer — has demanded gardens in the air, multiple exposures within an individual apartment, or the preservation of broad access to public amenities. To most people, such demands seem unattainable, fantastical, or utopian. And they appear inconsistent with the popular developers' axiom that the simpler the massing and the more cube-like the envelope, the greater the economy. Manipulating structural systems to create cantilevers or terraces, roof gardens, or cavities within the volume of the building increases labor, design, and material costs. Indeed, to give each apartment two, three, or four orientations means more exterior wall, more corners, more insulation — and a commensurately higher price.

The basic need to stack and cluster housing units arises from the desire to live in cities. By reconsidering the apartment tower from first principles, we would amplify tremendously the opportunities offered by urbanity. For everyone a garden, for everyone a penthouse, for everyone a view — these ambitions are surely not considered "economical" in a mathematical sense, or within the reach of most people, in the practical sense. But what has been considered economically sound in the past thirty years may prove, in the long term, to be more sociologically, politically, and even financially costly than we ever imagined.

CHAPTER 7

Confronting Mega-Scale

The Impact of Scale

In 1900 there were 3.4 million people in New York City. Today there are 7.3 million. There were 345,000 people in Mexico City then; today there are almost 21 million. There were 1.8 million people in Tokyo then, and there are 27 million today.[1] Ebenezer Howard designed his "Garden Cities for Tomorrow" for a population of 30,000; sixty-six years later, a *single* housing project in the Bronx (Co-op City) was designed for a population of 50,000. Today, a typical new Singapore town is built to house 200,000.

Today's tallest office building, the Scars Tower in Chicago, stands 1,454 feet in height, with 110 stories. In 1900, New York's St. Paul Building, standing 26 stories high, was one of the tallest buildings in the world. In 1900 there were 8,000 cars in the United States. There are 143 million today. Columbia University's enrollment was 2,208 then; today, it is almost 20,000. London's famous Burlington Arcade had 54 shops and 22 open stands. The West Edmonton Mall in Alberta, Canada, has over 800 shops, 20,000 parking places, and 5.2 million square feet of commercial space.[2]

These are not merely statistics, innocent indications of

expanding population or urbanization. Rather, they are signs that this century's population growth, and its convergence into giant metro-cities, has created an entirely new scale of development, a scale that has generically changed the nature and character of our institutions and the structures built to house them.

Mega-Scale and the Designer

We experience the disorientation of mega-scale regularly on our highways, in parking structures and in airports, in shopping malls and discount "superstores." At extremes, we see it in such cities as Tokyo and in such institutions as the Metropolitan Museum of Art.

Any trip to the hospital today will reveal how changes in the scale of medical practice have created entirely new kinds of experiences for all of us; the difference between a small-town forty-bed hospital and today's mega-hospital with several buildings and thousands of beds is not merely size, but also nature. Technology facilitates preparation and distribution of food and drugs, medical support systems, even the equipment used to practice medicine. Computerization and miniaturization have made it possible to control information flow: patient registration, hospital menus, and medical records. "Processing" thousands of patients every day, mega-hospitals are streamlined for efficiency with complete disregard for patients' comfort, privacy, or family members. In order to operate, such an institution must develop fundamentally new methods for people to move, congregate, operate, and confer. Although we are familiar enough with sophisticated organization and technology, we have little considered the enormous psychological and environmental impact of these changes, or the urgent demand for an architecture that can respond.

Some of the architectural implications are practical. For

example, how are we to gain a sense of orientation in a mega-project, find our way around the many wings and departments of an enormous complex? We have become all too familiar with today's endless array of signs and color codes. At one time, we passed through a public entrance and headed straight for the main gallery of the museum, the public reception room at the Pentagon, or the main lecture hall of the university — these were the spaces announced outside by the gilded dome or windowed barrel vault. Today, we often enter through the double doors, only to pursue a red or yellow line down corridors and around corners.

We know from old cities that techniques for creating hierarchy, amplified by an appropriate architectural vocabulary, can give us our bearings. Today's large complexes demand the development of hierarchy and an articulation of parts we would take for granted in a small building or town. A system of major interior "streets," smaller passages, and private "alleys," for example, could break down a complex building into comprehensible components. Distinctive architecture could then make each part recognizable and distinct within the whole. With countless new mega-plexes to design, we must recognize that in many cases, the building has become a city, and the task of an architect, inherently, that of a city planner.

A more subtle issue of building scale has to do with a sense of personal identity: what is our psychological mind-set as we compare our bodies to the size of the structures around us? Consider living in a house in a village. Clusters of smaller dwellings — even if compact — compare closely enough to the size of our own houses and bodies to give us a sense of location: we can automatically project ourselves into our surroundings. This is profoundly different from the feeling of a resident of the fifteenth floor of a sixty-story apartment tower, one of twenty-five such towers compactly clustered, as in a Singapore new town or the suburbs of São Paulo. A five-foot-tall person who walks among man-made structures one hundred times taller than he or she, who dwells behind a square in a repetitive facade — one of a dozen identical facades — is bound to feel diminished and lost.

Consider an office worker at the turn of the century, before the advent of air-conditioning. Working at a desk in a room with a window, he would have shared the space with three to fifteen other people. When hot, he might open the window, or when bored, call down to an acquaintance crossing the street below. How different is this experience when the building floor plate grows to one acre in size, is filled with hundreds of identical cubicles that block eye contact and vision to the outdoors, and then replicates vertically into the air, fifty, sixty, or seventy floors high? How different does it feel to enter and exit this building, to work with hundreds or thousands of people breathing the same processed air without access to daylight — one person in a thousand, in the same cube of air for cycles of days, months, and years?

These dilemmas are not, of course, rooted fundamentally in architecture or the art of building. They are dilemmas of the structure of our society, its economy, and its methods of organization, of humanity reproducing out of control — two, four, six, eight billion in population and still on the rise — with almost half of this number concentrated in metropolitan cities globally. Thus, public policy specialists have written on the necessity of stabilizing or decreasing the birth rate so that our human population might better relate to the earth's resources; social scientists have critiqued the evolution of multinational corporations, whose visions of efficiency demand vast, minimal, and rudimentary working facilities. And architects have responded to mega-scale by trying to camouflage it, attempting to ignore it, or adopting it wholeheartedly.

Architects React

A decade ago, postmodernist architects specialized in surface treatments that were aimed, in part, at counteracting the inherently new nature of mega-scale in the architectural program. Devoting much effort to composing the curtain wall from multiple materials and tints of glass, the designer would create complexity in the building envelope, simply accepting the inflated space inside. It was as if architects were more troubled by the scale of buildings as objects, and less by the gigantic spaces they held. Zigzags of color as on military airplanes or ships made forty-story buildings into assemblies of parts. Decorated skyscrapers came alive, like textiles, with pattern.

As we've seen, another group of architects has confronted the problem more recently by redefining it. Leon Krier has perched charming classical towns on hilltops; his brother Rob Krier has created urbane scenes of streets lined with five-story structures; Duany Plater-Zyberk has built charming pre-industrial villages; Walt Disney Co., with Robert A. M. Stern, Jacquelin Robertson, and others, has built a new town with the theme name "Celebration" — all of which completely ignore contemporary conditions of population, commerce, and transportation.

To propose that the new problems of scale can be restructured and reversed in order to return us to pre-industrial settlement patterns and nineteenth-century building types requires a high measure of wishful thinking, and, to an architect or planner confronted with the reality of urban North America and the developing world, is quite baffling. Knowingly or unknowingly, these designers rely on social, economic, and political conditions that cannot by any reasonable measure of realism be seriously considered obtainable in the face of the urban ills affecting the vast majority of the global population: ever-increasing densities, diminishing environmental and land resources, hugely scaled manufacturing and retail facilities, increasing car ownership, traffic, and parking needs. For an architect in Singapore, Hong Kong, or Tokyo contemplating new residential communities of hundreds of thousands of people, each of an average density of fifty to one hundred units per acre, the problem of scale is real: it is the result of fundamental changes to the statistical condition of humanity. And in this context, the argument that it can be avoided by "rearrangement" appears naive and misdirected.

The mega-school, whose most articulate spokesperson is Rem Koolhaas, recognizes and accepts the realities that are creating a mega-world of mega-buildings and mega-cities. In the face of "apocalyptic demographics . . . [and] the seeming failure of the urban," writes Koolhaas, "we have to dare to be utterly uncritical."[3] The architectural translation of this acceptance, in Koolhaas's projects for a proposed library at the University of Paris in Jussieu, the Congrexpo at Lille, and others, is a cacophony of juxtaposed forms and materials, loosely related parts, and a certain tentativeness toward building materials and forms. Koolhaas accepts our huge-scale, century's end alienation at face value, and amplifies it into a new kind of aesthetic. "Urbanism," he writes, "will not only, or mostly, be a profession, but a way of thinking, an ideology: to accept what exists. We were making sand castles. Now we swim in the sea that swept them away . . ."[4]

Beneath all of this lies resignation, the root conviction that these forces are bigger than us: that we cannot fight or harness them. Even more profoundly, any attempt to get to their deeper meaning, to act critically, to seek order, or to intervene is tantamount to assuming an inappropriate power in the context of today's pluralistic democracy. "It would require," Koolhaas writes, "a second innocence to believe, at the end of the twentieth century, that the urban — the built — can be planned and mastered."[5]

The deep pessimism in this attitude toward mega-scale is concealed in a kind of joyous acceptance of what is emerging, not unlike the manner in which some architects embraced "pop" mass culture several decades ago. But mass culture, of course, is a misnomer for mega-scale. It is not mass culture that is being displayed, but the uncontrolled, rampant emergence of a post-industrial consumer economy gone mad — pouring into cities in every part of the world, growing at an enormous rate, and consuming limited, precious resources. In this reality, we — humanity in general, and architects in particular — become instruments of mega-scale's raw expression.

True, the forces causing mega-scale are overwhelming, and they appear irreversible, at least for a few generations to come. The undifferentiated, relentlessly repetitive workspaces, the windowless environments, the cacophony of industrial structures, the gigantic, repetitive assemblage of apartment towers — these are the uninhibited results of forces larger than an individual architect, corporate trader, international businessperson, or citizen, and of patterns that simply did not exist in the era of the New England town or the gentle, classical city. We must, with the mega-school, agree that changing technology, information transfer, social structures, demographics, mobility requirements, and economic forces are shaping the environment in which we live.

But to decide that we are innocent and helpless bystanders is surely no response worthy of us as a society. As architects, if we are to be compassionate and identify with those for whom we build — those navigating through vast parking structures, insecure and alienated; those driving through urban landscapes of nonexistent buildings screened by parking structures and the

blank back walls of shops — the only path is to attempt to understand the forces of mega-scale, to appreciate the need for new
architectural inventions, and to intervene, in search of a more
humane, spiritually uplifting, and unoppressive environment.

The Role of the Architect

The architectural program for a building today, without stren-
uous intervention on the part of the designer, often directly
translates into an endlessly repetitive maze of internal passages,
public corridors, football fields of manufacturing functions,
and indoor office "landscapes." Mega-scale must be recognized
as a paradigm shift that inevitably challenges the basic assumptions of architecture.

The organization and hierarchy of circulation, the articulation of the component parts within the whole, the
manipulation of forms and masses to maximize exposure to the
outside, the refinement of interior and exterior relationships,
the moderation of the building's scale as experienced in the city:
these are all architectural means of addressing fundamental
aspects of human perception. Given the assignment to design a
mega-facility, architects must apply their professional expertise meaningfully to engage the growing tyranny of size.

To start, we must critically evaluate the assumptions that lead
to super-scaled places. We might solve traffic congestion by creating wider roads, or we might consider ways to eliminate the
need for so many car trips in the first place. When new cities and
towns are built, as in Singapore, Hong Kong, Israel, and other
parts of the world, the notion that we must build at very great
densities is often taken for granted; it is natural to do so in downtown land that is very expensive and desirable. But why should
these assumptions of high density be taken for granted? In some
cases, by consuming more land initially, we might preserve more

open space in the long term. One way to diffuse mega-scale, certainly, is to rethink its basic premise.

Architects cannot solve everything, but we can and must ask the right questions. Before we build structures to hold thousands of work cubicles on a single floor, we should be asking how many people *require* being in the same building, or on a single, continuous floor, to complete a task effectively? Before building yet another wing of a mega-hospital, why not ask ourselves whether one mega-hospital is preferable to half a dozen specialized facilities? Might we be better served by a complex of pavilions, and if so, should they be joined in a sequence side by side, or one on top of the other? Should there be twenty patients around a nursing station, or fifty? Should there be ten people in a room, or two? What degree of privacy can be maintained for a patient? Under what conditions might patients want to interact with their families? These are questions most often resolved on a purely economic basis. Yet they are also architectural decisions of consequence, and we cannot continue to analyze the costs and benefits of a design without considering the qualitative, three-dimensional consequences of decisions such as these.

The role of an architect, therefore, must be to actively question assumptions from a spatial point of view. In each case, the architect should help weigh the cost-effectiveness of building decisions against human comfort, well-being, even dignity, over the building's lifetime. Certain features, such as larger or more numerous windows, might cost more. Others, such as maximizing southern exposures for living spaces, have no bearing on cost whatsoever. Still others might even save money, such as designing a hospital room to provide opportunities for family members themselves to care for patients.

Because of our particular knowledge of, and sensitivity to,

these issues, we architects must become vocal participants in developing the programs for projects we build — since these initial programs themselves generate many of our basic and widespread problems. It is essential that architects deal with the problem of scale both as critics and as creators: first, by looking at the program and its fundamental assumptions critically, and second, by actively understanding the spatial implications, architects should bring their skills to bear in designing formal solutions that truly speak to the impact of scale.

THE SUPERCONDUCTING SUPER COLLIDER LABORATORY
In 1993, I was paid a surprise visit in my Boston office by Roy Schwitters, director of the Superconducting Super Collider Laboratory (SSC) in Waxahachie, Texas, accompanied by my friend, Harvard physicist Melissa Franklin. Schwitters was in the midst of planning and design work for the Laboratory. On the scientific side, excavation had begun on the fifty-four-mile-long tunnel that would accommodate the accelerators and colliders under the Texas plains. Groups of scientists were busy designing the test installations, some of them the size of a large airplane hangar. In Waxahachie, well over one thousand scientists were at work, installed in two giant warehouse buildings converted "temporarily" for this use. It was time, Schwitters explained, to turn to planning the human facilities: the campus, laboratories, and housing for the three thousand people who would be part of this project once the tunnels were complete and the experiment was launched.

Schwitters had heard of my earlier visit to the Fermilab near Chicago, and of my criticism of its design, a high-rise lab tower set in a vast expanse of land, as inappropriate for the endeavor it was planned to hold. He came with open questions. What kind of place should the SSC be? Should there be a centralized campus? How might interaction among diverse members of the community be encouraged? We spoke of other scientific communities — Stanford (SLAC), Geneva (CERN) — where great laboratories existed, and what did and did not work there.

By day's end, Schwitters invited me to come to Waxahachie and meet with the planning group; I was to take on the responsibility for master planning and designing the campus. As I traveled south, I had a romantic vision of what awaited me: one of the greatest teams of scientists ever assembled working intensively under one roof (actually, it was two).

A twenty-minute drive south from downtown Dallas, a giant converted warehouse called "Building Four" stood in a cluster of other industrial buildings housing the laboratory. With an area of 100,000 square feet, Building Four was a single-story structure, and with the exception of one wall of offices, windowless. With four hundred physicists, engineers, technicians, and support staff at work in identical little cubicles, it was impossible to find someone without a map in hand.

A few miles closer to Waxahachie and the accelerator tunnel was a so-called "central facility" — another warehouse (a former Sears Roebuck distribution center) more recently converted to handle the overflow SSC personnel from Building Four. "Central" had an area of 500,000 square feet and accommodated one thousand people, each without exception assigned to a cubicle in another endless,

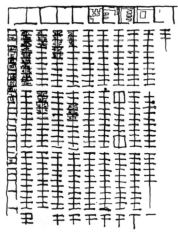

Segment of SCC "central facility" with work stations

artificially lit space. As an outsider stumbling upon the scene, I wondered how these individuals — leading physicists and scientists from around the world — could tolerate this totally dehumanized and disorienting environment. After just one day, I felt dizzy and humiliated by the succession of meetings in windowless rooms and total lack of daylight in this vast, oppressive environment.

Some months later, I developed a plan for the SSC campus with the architects in my Boston office. In order to create a strong sense of place in the flat prairie, we organized the campus around a large pond necessary to regulate the temperature of the Collider, created by damming a small stream on the site. Our objective was to design diverse workspaces of labs, private studies, and offices; to provide housing for those who came for brief periods; and to create a strong center where all common facilities would be clustered. On one side of the pond, we planned laboratories and offices protruding into the water, endowed with generous daylight and views onto the prairie; on the opposite side, a hotel and education center, and in between, joining each shore of the pond, a bridge-building containing the cafeteria, library, meeting rooms, auditorium, and electronic control rooms. Accessible both to scientists and the public at large, the double-height wing constituted a kind of downtown street along which everyone would meet.

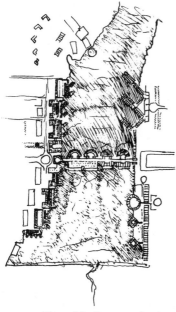

Plan of the Superconducting Super Collider Campus

In presentations to the group of physicists, staff, and officials from the Department of Energy (which was funding the
project), we illustrated how the campus might act as a catalyst
for the interaction of the thousands of individuals taking part
in this great experiment. Many partaking in the discussions
were skeptical that an environment of such quality could be
achieved. Indeed, a group of scientists on the frontiers of
knowledge, trying to discover a unified theory to explain all
of the workings of nature, was unable to comprehend that it
might be possible to achieve a wholesome and uplifting work
environment! But as models and drawings were elaborated
and presented for group discussion, an excitement set in. Our
models of ponds, gardens, and articulated three-story structures overlooking the water contrasted bizarrely with the space
within Building Four where we were presenting the material.

The government officials involved, particularly those
from the Department of Energy, were not only skeptical, but
almost cynical, and their doubts were only to be confirmed
in the summer of 1993, when the House of Representatives
voted against continuing the SSC. At the ensuing congres-
sional hearings, the debate was not about architecture and
the campus. It was about Big Science and the $8 billion
needed to try to find the basic building blocks of nature.
Undoubtedly, much of the debate was precipitated by the fact
that the Cold War was over, and with no direct or indirect
benefit for national defense, the pure scientific research represented by the SSC was bound to suffer a blow.

But although the debate centered on science and its costs
per se — the committee did not spare the issue of the physical environment and the projected campus plan for the SSC.
Reviewing the $8 billion outlay for the experiment, the com-
mittee was critical of the cost of some potted plants that had

been purchased to relieve the dismal existing facility, and in time, they came to ask about the cost of the architectural model of the SSC campus — not the cost of the campus, but of the *model*. Word had gotten out, apparently, that a "glamorous" scheme had been developed for the campus.

I reflected how typical it was that a group of elected representatives would consider that two thousand scientists working in windowless warehouses was a responsible use of public funds. Sensitive to any possible accusations of "wastefulness," politicians felt compelled to reject the idea of building a humane workspace to serve the scientific community at the SSC for the decades to come. It became clear that in the public psyche, a well-endowed working environment is deemed to be a luxury and an impropriety, whereas an oppressive, mean environment represents an appropriate gesture of fiscal responsibility.

The Role of the Public

At the beginning of this century, adherents of the Progressive and City Beautiful Movements took to the streets, the newspapers, and magazines to protest, with great indignation, against inhumane conditions in the industrializing cities where they lived. In Chicago and New York, in particular, numerous voices called for action to improve qualities they found substandard in the urban spaces provided for living, working, and gathering: darkness and poor ventilation in tenement buildings, crowding and exploitation in industrial sweatshops, the lack of public parks or a well-maintained public realm. Today, we take equivalent types of environmental deprivation for granted.

We are clearly facing a conflict between the reality of growing numbers of individuals who must be fed, housed, employed, and cared for, and the innate human desire for the measure of comfort derived from interacting with a relatively small, familiar group. As of yet evolution has shown no signs of decreasing our visceral response to the forest, the open countryside, and the village — and against massive buildings of mega-scale. Critical analysis and evolution notwithstanding, however, the problem of mega-scale is real. To mitigate the chaos that has long been augured will require new inventions, new design methodologies, and unprecedented solutions.

PART III

TOWARD THE FUTURE

CHAPTER 8
Planning the Region

Making Places

A memorable place often occupies an important feature in the landscape: a harbor, a bay, a river delta, a lake, a hill within a town — a physical event in the natural environment. We remember places that are dignified by a unique interaction between the man-made and the natural, places like Naples by the bay, Geneva at the lake's end, Rome on the Tiber's bend, Cape Town with Table Mountain, Amsterdam and its canals, or Ronda, Spain, a city bridging between two cliffs. Not only are these places set in special points in the landscape, but their own construction often amplifies their surroundings: an alignment of buildings on the watershed to overlook views (Jerusalem), buildings that contain the curve of a harbor (Cannes), an important bridge to cross a river (the Ponte Vecchio). Great urban streets frequently maintain specific relationships to the natural terrain (Barcelona's Ramblas descending to the bay) and link the most intense urban activity with great parks and gardens (Fifth Avenue in New York City, the Champs Elysées in Paris, or Regent Street in London).

What we recognize as the special character of a city is the synthesis of an identifiable spatial structure with the unique mysteries and secrets of its site. As we know, many urban centers share the same generic diagram (a grid or radiating boulevards, for example) but differ enormously from one another. Differences of culture, scale, and architectural vocabulary all contribute to making cities particular, yet truly singular places are often characterized by an unusually close interaction between the builders' ideals and the specific character of their terrain. Fundamental to developing a sense of place is the art of recognizing and seizing upon the very special, sometimes subtle, features over which an urban diagram is laid.

In the past, survival had much to do with this commitment to investigating and discovering the best place to build. Conditioned by necessities of defense (hilltops or cliffs as at Masada), effective transportation (rivers, valleys, harbors, or canals as in Venice or Amsterdam), sources of water, fertile land, the availability of building materials, or even mystical issues of geometry and orientation, the construction of urban and rural settlements was initiated by an almost sacred act of planning. Thus were cities and villages born of a plan, a structure, a social contract — even a covenant — intended to chart the future.

Little of such consideration has occurred in the development of the regional city. With the heavy hand of today's technologies exerted against nature, the constraints of old have disappeared; the development process today is almost ruthlessly predictable. In redeveloped cities (such as Stamford), as well as in entirely new developing regions, the process begins with numerous developers operating independently. They start by exploring all reasonably priced land zoned for their particular segment of urban activity. In a vacuum of public input or professional cooperation, each developer is concerned with a specialized component of development: office or manufacturing, shopping center or housing. One of the principal criteria is proximity to a major transportation corridor and the opportunity for automobile access. The second criterion is ample and cheap parking. In less developed regional locations, the built development will often begin with a mall sited at a cloverleaf between two interstate highways. Office parks and shopping centers immediately follow, replacing woods, fields, and views.

Rarely does the placement of a road recognize the natural potential of the land it makes accessible, since freeway alignments, punctuated by their rhythm of intersections and cloverleafs, are based purely on aerial photographs and engineering analysis of optimal routes between various points. Nor can we identify a single suburban shopping mall whose location was chosen specifically to take advantage of a special feature of the land. Instead, everywhere we look, we see rolling hillsides bulldozed flat to facilitate the "efficient" construction of suburban tract houses; valleys filled in as giant parking lots for shopping mall sites; rivers culverted and covered to avoid the complications of surface drainage and maintenance. Our modern capacity to overcome any formation of nature is currently exercised by habit, blindly disrupting our dwindling natural resources and destroying the idiosyncratic topography that once made each place unique.

MODI'IN

The key to designing a building, for me, is discovering the secrets of a site — the ways in which the land cues a design to suggest the building's organization and form. This applies to designing a building within an existing city, where the pattern of streets, neighboring structures, architectural heritage, and culture all constitute the site, or to designing a project sited in the open landscape, where the shapes of the topography can generate form.

In 1988, I was asked to develop the plan for a brand new city — Modi'in — to be built in Israel in the foothills halfway between Tel Aviv and Jerusalem. Although the region was the place of the ancient city of Modi'in of the Maccabees some two thousand years ago, the land then consisted of a series of bare hills and valleys oriented east–west with respect to the Mediterranean Sea.

As I began thinking about Modi'in, I was preoccupied with the notion of other new cities — those built in recent decades both in Israel and abroad — and what might be learned from their successes and failures. The new cities built in Israel since the inception of the State drew upon the same concepts that had guided most cities of the post–Second World War era — Brasilia, Chandigarh (the new capital of Punjab designed by Le Corbusier), and the many new towns built in England and elsewhere in Europe. Common to all of them was the belief that a city should be made up of relatively autonomous neighborhoods, each provided with local services such as shops, schools, and community centers. With these services generally placed in the heart of the neighborhood, a super-grid of arterial roads was then imposed on the plan so that each area would be well served by highways to carry heavy traffic around the perimeter. Somewhere within this super-grid, one great square would be dedicated as the urban center. This layout was applied as readily to towns in flat desert areas as to those nestled into rugged hillsides.

Today, the new Israeli communities of the 1950s and 1960s have deteriorated. Ignoring most landscape features existing on the site has erased any sense of identity or individual character for these new towns, and with edges defined by arterial roads, wide, lonely gaps were created between communities. Lacking variety, disconnected from each other and from any civic center, the disunified developments have produced a sterile conglomeration of dormitory-like communities.

Such modern planned cities are based on concepts of discontinuity. With only highways to "connect" neighborhoods, and dead-end streets or *cul-de-sacs* to "protect" the residents from thru-traffic, no continuous network of thoroughfares is possible. In traditional cities, evolved over time, neighborhoods overlap and the borders between them are ambiguous. Neighborhood centers are located along an arterial road that extends from one neighborhood through the next, and on to the city center. These "normal cities," as I came to call them, were often based in part on a simple grid, and they prospered on continuity.

While I did not think that a grid was the appropriate response to Modi'in's complex topography, a continuous hierarchical network was essential to connect the city. I came to think of designing Modi'in as the task of preserving the qualities of a "normal city," while responding to the contemporary needs of transportation and mobility.

With these objectives in mind I turned to the site, recognizing patterns in the valleys as they linked to form larger valleys and contain hills in between. I had known from other new towns built in hilly terrain that valleys inevitably become the domain of the highway planners. It is there they can place roads most conveniently, and thus, on the hilltops and slopes, create neighborhoods as separate enclaves. In Modi'in, this model would only perpetuate the precedent of a discontinuous city, where it is impossible to walk from one neighborhood to another, where the separation of communities would kill any potential for urban vitality.

Driving by Jeep through the treeless land, I also wondered how we might make this city a garden city, a green place. The rich topsoil that had gathered in the valleys would surely be the easiest place to plant trees, to create a natural network of parks and playgrounds, together with community facilities. It struck me then that the valleys of Modi'in might be the key to the solution; they must carry traffic, I thought, but not via highways. The valleys, thirty to one hundred yards wide, could become "green rivers": lavishly planted, with parks, schools, neighborhood shops, and community facilities contained by a couplet of one-way roads on either side. These roads, resembling grand-scale boulevards, would define the valleys' edges, and housing would extend up each slope of the hill.

I became determined that the city would preserve the forms of the land, protecting the places of exceptional beauty and archeology, and making plant life an integral part of its design. It was essential that the construction both of roads and of buildings not reshape the topography.

Back in the studio, we made a large model of the entire site. At a scale of 1:2,500, it was made up of fifty one-meter-square modules, and it filled a large room. Working directly with building blocks of foam-core, we designed the housing to follow the slope of the land and to rise only up to four stories in height, just within the tops of trees. As the hills sloped, the buildings terraced down with them. I knew that without special care, roads would be cut into the land as a matter of habit, wiping out hilltops and filling in valleys. Therefore, we fit the roads into the model's topography ourselves with minimum earthwork, and designed tall buildings as landmarks on the landscaped hilltops: housing with distant views toward the Mediterranean and the hills of Jerusalem.

Integrating the function of an arterial road with the civic scale and identity of an urban boulevard, the valley roads would define the spine or lifeline of the community as a kind of river of urban activity and open space. Where neighborhood roads intersected with the valley roads,

A Modi'in valley

neighborhood centers would occur, with clustered shopping, local offices, clinics, community services, and schools. As a whole, the mixed-use district of each valley seemed to create the kind of synergy we associate with the vital urban life of "normal" cities.

The valleys of Modi'in and their neighborhoods meander through the topography, and at their confluence, the heart of the city occurs: the "downtown," or urban center. Natural, central gathering places, the valleys are visible from the neighborhoods on the surrounding hilly slopes, and like traditional centers, they combine a variety of functions — a route of travel, places for shopping, education, and recreation. Free of those aspects of street that Le Corbusier so vehemently rejected, they become a public place for the community, and integrate street and urban park into a new form. Lavishly planted and irrigated, each valley is planted with specific species to enhance its individual character — the

Valley of the Pines, the Palms, the Jacarandas, and so on.

In the heart of the city, extending westward from the city center, runs the existing Wadi Anaba valley. Typical for the area, the Wadi forms steeply sloped natural terracing, which in many places was extended with retaining walls built into the natural rock layers by ancient farmers. Filled with water in the rainy winter, but dry in the summer, the crevice of the valley changes from a deep green filled with wild flowers and trees, to a dry and thorny wheat color over the seasons of a year. Set aside as a nature preserve of biblical rocky cliffs and sparse olive and carob trees, the Wadi will remain an untouched resource for residents of the city.

In 1996, the first residents moved into Modi'in. As palm trees were being planted in the first valley, children were arriving at the valley schools, descending from the houses on the hills — pioneers of the city to be: projected population, 200,000.

Recent Patterns of Development

In the great urban expansion of recent decades, two distinct patterns of development predominate. Within traditional city centers, well-established city planning departments, redevelopment authorities, and often strong constituencies of interested parties have brought some degree of public interest to bear on new development. Developers would be the first to admit that written zoning and urban design guidelines are only part of the set of forces they must confront in undertaking any major downtown project. In downtown San Francisco, New York, Boston, Philadelphia, and even Los Angeles, developers must face, in addition to regulatory guidelines, a number of quasi-official and less predictable procedures: evaluations by appointed community consultation boards and citizen action groups; required approvals by historic district boards and environmental protection organizers; and/or litigation by neighborhood associations and private interests.

In contrast, a major project in the outlying regional city often faces a regulatory *tabula rasa* — in which the only issues of concern to the developer are locating vast undeveloped parcels of land, easy highway access, and captive populations — all "regulated" only by the forces of the market. There is rarely any preexisting urban pattern to fit into, few neighboring residents to placate, and no history or memory to constrain design.

Even when the project is enormous and its environmental impact potentially very significant, the developer usually confronts only a county government with little power or a small municipality eager for major investment (and a new tax base). Opposition to an individual development by environmental or no-growth lobbies can often be overcome by the sheer power of investment capital. And because a large proportion of new development occurs in relatively sparsely populated areas, there is seldom an established constituency to express its views, even though within a decade or two the center could serve hundreds of thousands of people. Of course, by this time every architectural, economic, planning, and land-use decision already will have become a fact of life.

For more than a century we have thought of the urban realm as primarily the city core and, perhaps, its innermost suburbs. Land beyond the immediate periphery of the downtown, where the majority of developers now and for many years have been investing and building, has been recognized, perhaps, as "developing" (and therefore, in progress) — not as a place of immediate relevance. The farther away it lies from existing centers, the less likely such development is to draw any attention or planning intervention; in other words, the place most directly affected by new construction is conveniently yet to be built.

Nor, as we have seen, are individual developers motivated to consider their developments as part of an urban whole. Sensitive specifically to vehicular connections, developers are generally indifferent to the notion that if combined with other developments, the sum might be greater than the individual, and in most cases, isolated parts. Thus, each development is unto itself: a world with its own rules.

Development outside the historic city centers has suffered because there has simply been very little or no attempt whatsoever to plan the environment comprehensively. Land-use planning — the conservation of agriculture or open green space and zoning for new development — has been generated almost entirely at the local level. In North America, farsighted land-use planning at the scale of the expanded city has been practically nonexistent: no proactive regional strategy designates certain areas for development, others for conservation and green belts, others for preservation as agricultural land.

The only reasonable excuse for this situation can be the fact that we have not yet recognized the regional city as an integrated formal, social, or political entity. The greatest resistance to regional administration has been raised by the individual small towns and peripheral centers that make up the region itself. Development that would strengthen an entire region is often opposed by local residents who perceive any move toward regional unity as a threat to their own mandate. Because many towns and cities derive as much as 75 percent of their tax revenues from tax on property,[1] local land-use decisions are enormously relevant to property owners and municipal governments alike, with tensions arising frequently between the need to seek revenue and the desire to protect a lifestyle that drew residents away from downtown in the first place.

By distributing authority to the most local levels, we tend to believe we can increase our control, remembering this or that disastrous highway project that was stopped by local opposition, saving a neighborhood or a coastline. What has become clear, however, is that local government is potent in stopping projects — in saying "no" — but has proven entirely unable to develop consensus, let alone action, in *implementing* any broad project or program. Even projects considered generally in the public good — building a mass transit line to an airport, creating a national or regional park, or developing a coordinated plan for various elements of public transportation and roads — produce endless controversy. Therefore, we more comfortably defer to the power of the veto than take positive action.

The problem is also administrative: metro-regions grow without respect to any existing legislative borders. While many municipalities proclaim autonomy, and hence the right to self-determination, most have become inextricably part of an expanded city. Woven into the culture of the region, residents of these enclaves choose their places of work and recreation from a broad range of possibilities; they benefit from what the entire region has to offer — its services, and its cultural and commercial facilities. They also benefit from the hospitals and enjoy the higher education provided in the expanded city around them. Finally, they rely upon and at the same time are financially, socially, and politically affected by regional road systems, public transportation networks, and shared infrastructure. Thus, because contemporary communities are developing across municipal government lines, no institution wields the power to enact a comprehensive development strategy — even if such were desired.

For this reason, only a complete reorientation of public thinking about the significance and long-term impact of *every* development in the regional city, no matter how isolated it is in the short term or how unrelated to existing patterns of settlement, will create from today's disjointed environment a cohesive and coherent regional city in the future.

Central Planning

The 1980s and 1990s in North America mark two decades of particular disengagement from, and suspicion of, planning cities — new and old. The broad visions of modernist urbanism, so indelibly marked in the minds of designers around the world from the 1930s into the 1950s, depended upon a powerful central planning entity. And we have grown to associate many of the catastrophes of real-life projects (like the now crime-infested Robert Taylor homes in Chicago or the now demolished Pruitt-Igoe housing in St. Louis) with an image of rampant power transforming entire neighborhoods, several broad strokes at a time. For when a powerful building authority errs, its mistakes can be both very large and very long-lasting. The mid-1960s Model Cities program, for example, planned whole neighborhoods as part of its effort at urban renewal, and federal block grants funded many of these projects. Central planning authorities at the time devised massive interventions in cities across the country that effectively bypassed the democratic involvement of the communities and citizens whom they directly affected. Although they were undertaken with great optimism, so many of those housing projects and freeways devastated our cities and demolished our neighborhoods that the entire enterprise has been, with hindsight, discredited.

While some have criticized these projects as motivated less by idealism than by prejudice (cleaning up neighborhoods by clearing out their populations), the central failure of these projects was not intrinsically their scale or social intentions, but their design methods. They intentionally replaced an authentic urban fabric with new precincts of few streets, no public domain, and towers floating in flat, open space that constituted an urban vacuum. Having so recently witnessed this almost universal failure of central planning, therefore, when it comes to real estate, our distrust of comprehensive urban planning today is profound.

Above all, there has been a suspicion in the United States, especially, that any comprehensive type of urban planning is merely, and inherently, an authoritarian act and an extension of "Big Government." As deregulation occurred in many fields — banking, aviation, trucking — there also emerged the idea that deregulating the city planning and development process would result in a system shaped purely by the market, which, it was thought, would produce more efficient and responsive development. Meanwhile, over the last two decades, most cities have introduced a battery of public review requirements, environmental impact statements, and community planning boards into the development process — a system of checks and balances — as a "democratic" way to prevent "mistakes."

The notion of central planning, therefore, has been attacked and eroded from both directions: by introducing disunified methods of public intervention on the one hand, and on the other, by assuming that the marketplace, without comprehensive guidance, is an effective tool for creating workable cities.

This is not to say that the United States, in particular, has never resorted to central planning. Certainly, the production of vital goods during the world wars was centrally controlled, as were prices, and the Tennessee Valley Authority, founded in 1933 and fully funded by the federal government, provided cheap hydroelectric power to towns all over the American South. When it came to the construction of the interstate highway system in the 1950s, considerable central planning, federal financing, and coordination were undertaken and supported, and today, supervision of the airways and the sky, even outer space, is centrally planned.

Indeed, it could be argued that some of the greatest achievements of American technology and initiative have been the result of central planning, carefully camouflaged. Perhaps the most dramatic example is the planning undertaken in the design and implementation of the national and international telephone systems. Here, to avoid the intervention of a national planning authority, as in the case of the PTT national post office and telephone networks of Europe, a monopoly was created (AT&T and the Bell system in the United States) to allow a private-sector company enough incubation time and latitude to plan and finance the entire national phone system. Only with the system in place and fully coordinated have its ownership and management been broken down into several competing entities — a tacit admission, perhaps, that real solutions demand some form of centralized planning.

The Limits of the Market

Only recently have we begun to question our now long-standing assumption that a flourishing free market economy would also generate rational and desirable urban form. To be sure, private development generated considerable expansion during the 1980s — much of which occurred not downtown, but in the regional city. In 1991, in his book *Edge City*, Joel Garreau heralded the sprawling suburban centers as "a vigorous world rising far from the old downtowns, where little save villages or farmland lay only thirty years before."[2] The book, a favorite among developers, argues that by allowing uninhibited business-people to act in a free marketplace, we have brought about a new city that closely conforms to the aspirations of most Americans.

Of all metropolitan regions, Houston, Texas, has been, perhaps, the least constricted in recent years by grand plans. With
a local development slogan of "no zoning" whatsoever, Houston
embodies every urban ill found in metropolitan cities. And as
architect Deyan Sudjic puts it, in the resulting free-for-all environment, "you feel an emptiness everywhere."[3] What is in
question today is our confidence in the fundamental processes
of representative democracy. Without some form of coopera-
tive, comprehensive planning, we find the widespread
disappearance of public open space, habitable parks, and natural
amenities downtown and out of town alike.

MONTREAL

In the heart of Montreal stands Mount Royal Park, created in
1877 and designed by Frederick Law Olmsted, today serving
a regional city of 3.1 million people. A visit to the Montreal
archives, surprisingly, would reveal the lively debate that
occurred in connection with acquiring the land as a park. At
that time, Montreal comprised a population of about 112,000
and its city limits were bound by a line ten city blocks from
the river edge. One councilman after another protested that
buying this land so far from the city for a park was unlikely to
serve the citizens well — that it was too far to be useful.
Despite the opposition of the many powerful landowners
whose country mansions surrounded and populated the
mountain, the land was expropriated and the park established.
   Today the park is in the geographic heart of the most
intense development in the city. It is impossible to think of
Montreal without Mount Royal Park, but it is also obvious that
without the foresight of certain community leaders more than
one hundred years ago, creating the park would have been
impossible. Even within two or three decades of the decision

to establish the park, development pressures and increased land values would have made the expropriation of the land prohibitively expensive, and politically improbable.

Today, the decision to reserve several square miles as park for an entire city would antagonize landowners losing development options, conservatives opposing social spending, private corporations promoting downtown vitality, and any number of citizen interest groups. In the mood and political structure prevailing today, creating Central Park in New York City would be impossible.

Yet I am absolutely certain that projects equally significant as Central Park and Mount Royal Park exist today in every regional city, and clearly, these are opportunities that do not knock twice.

A New Case for Regional Planning

There are in many areas of the United States already models for "metro governments," as they are often called, which tacitly recognize that the future of our built environment is not a local-scale problem, but requires cooperation and foresight. Setting priorities and agendas for various types of planning at the regional scale, many agencies have started by addressing those issues most clearly demanding regional coordination — water and power grids; regional waste disposal; coordination of the regional road system; and in some cases, creation of a metropolitan transit authority. Recently, some of these agencies have expanded to deal with social and economic issues affecting a geographic region, like attracting new business development, providing low-interest home-ownership loans, and rebuilding regional infrastructure.[4] Regional restructuring has been gaining power in recent years, from the Municipality of Metropolitan Toronto to the Montreal Urban

Community; from the regional government of greater Vancouver to the State of Oregon.

It is relatively easy to imagine new concepts for greater mobility, equity, and control over land-use in our cities that could be implemented by a highly structured central authority with a broad mandate. But today in North America, to enact powerful central planning of urban development would require serious ideological and practical changes in our mindset. Our burden, instead, is to conceive new arrangements that are plausible in an environment delicately balancing a free market, a pluralistic society, and the rights of the individual on one side, and the best interests of the community on the other. We must create new conditions in which a vision of the city is integrated with feedback from the city's inhabitants, and in which a central authority is vested with power to enact this vision in a manner unthreatening to individuals or communities.

It is not in the nature of North American realpolitik to devise stringent regulatory schemes, even when the objective appears uncontroversial to create a vital, wholesome, economically viable public domain. In fact, the entire land development tradition in the United States is deeply rooted in the concept of individual land ownership, and it breeds a landowner who feels an intrinsic right to determine what might happen to his or her holdings.

Transportation Planning Is the Key

Any proposal for reshaping the city must include the means to take us from present conditions to the conditions we desire in the future. Therefore, we must consider those conditions of the new regional city that are already, necessarily, inherently public and that already involve and require broad cooperation. Transportation is the one central, shared concern of governing entities within one region. It is the one subject around which disparate municipal governments have real incentive to cooperate and rally.

As long as we continue to settle outside the boundaries of walking city centers, our dependence on mobility will remain constant or increase. Recognizing that transportation is intrinsically a regional concern, intrinsically connected with urban form, and therefore, a key to shaping and guiding regional land-use today, can transform our approach to planning the region.

Consider a special case in land development: the planning of resorts. For this particular land-use, the selection of a site and the role of transportation have always been reversed from the process we normally see in North America. In planning a resort, it would be inconceivable simply to build where a highway happened to be present. Instead, a careful survey across a coastline, a mountain range, or valley is conducted to identify the most attractive location; *then* a road, highway, airport, or railway link is constructed. This technique — first surveying the land for special places, and then designing the appropriate transportation system — should become a model for planning our regional cities.

To date, a multitude of agencies at different administrative levels have been responsible for regional transportation in the United States. This has been mostly "demand-side" planning: freeways are financed by federal, state, and local governments to alleviate congestion. City subway lines have been extended to reach newer suburbs years after they are sorely needed. From the federal government, Amtrak receives about 2 percent of the amount of money invested annually in roads, and in 1995, the national railway's budget was cut in half by Congress.[5] Regional trains, lacking popular "demand" and therefore financing, have scarcely been built at all. Today it is essential that we plan rapid rail and traditional or automated highways to link existing and expanding centers, and to no lesser extent, that we use these transportation systems to guide new development that is sensitive and appropriate to its location in the region.

As we develop new places, to discover and respond to the specificity of a building site will be as relevant to existing cities as it is to virgin land. Instead of depending upon market forces and independent local initiatives, we can establish the qualities we admire in the city by carefully, and strategically, planning public investment in infrastructure and transportation. As in the past, by rationalizing our transportation systems, we will create the opportunity for a new kind of city.

CHAPTER 9

Traveling the Region

Some have predicted that the dispersed city and its indispensable automobile will ultimately threaten our society's survival. Based on a premise that highly developed societies require the interaction provided by compact and concentrated cities, European planners, in particular, have argued that we must vigorously resist any further suburbanization. Our society and cities might then, with some luck and drastic measures, be served (and saved) by more affordable utilities, services, effective public transportation — and infused with a healthy level of human contact.

Yet we must not mistake cause for effect, the means from the motivating desire. The extensive suburban migration that has created our dispersed cities is not only a response to the growth and congestion in the city center, but also a profound cultural and psychological desire — omnipresent in North America — for freedom, expansiveness, privacy, and flexibility. For this reason, the post–Second World War suburban thrust in North America has continued to leap-frog and extend forever beyond existing urbanization. This core motivation represents a fundamental departure from the cultural and social mindset that has sustained traditional concentrated cities in other times and societies.

"If the Pope shaped Rome and the doge Venice and Baron Haussmann the *grands boulevards* of the Champs-Elysées," writer

Joel Garreau has pithily noted, "the marketplace rules Edge City."[1] This observation is partly true. The power of the real estate speculator over the pattern and shape of our cities past and present, as we have observed, should not be underestimated, and the broad and well-nurtured market for the automobile further ensures that distances can and will be traveled. But the public's deep desire for open space and unrestrained mobility is itself fueled by powerful cultural forces indeed. And the idea of a concentrated, intense city seems tolerable to us only when it is forever held in counterpoint to the dispersed city: open, without limits, bordering limitless land.

Policy for the coming decades cannot, therefore, rest on the premise of forcing a reversal of the desire to disperse. Rather, we should aim to facilitate and shape our wanderings, creating new centers of concentration within dispersed, leafy districts — in other words, designing the best of both worlds.

Transportation and the American Dream

To date, urban policies around the world have focused primarily either on concentration — in Europe or Singapore, for example — or dispersal, as in the United States. In North America, proponents of investing in our highway programs fundamentally seek to further what they perceive as the American Dream for a suburban lifestyle. Through highway construction, they support and amplify the components of dispersal — single-family houses, development of regional super-malls, convenient and affordable car travel — while dismissing the economies of scale and quality of life that have always resulted from concentration. Indeed, while much of the public might agree with the idea of developing a fast, convenient mass transportation system to supplement road travel, few would actually support any policy that appeared to limit their ability to use their own cars.

In contrast, proponents of the traditional city have advocated investment in all forms of mass transit, seeing well-developed alternatives to the car as the most potent tool in strengthening and revitalizing concentrated city centers. This group lobbies against investment in roads and fuel subsidies, which they see as merely encouraging further dispersal. Yet their argument is not only unrealistic, but also just as limited in scope as rejecting urban centers completely.

The most necessary, profound change in our visions is to recognize that only a variety of great concentrations strongly and permanently joined with expansive areas of dispersal will create for us the rich, accessible, diverse, communal, landscaped city we desire for our present and future. The future regional city must be a place where multiple centers of great density integrate work, commerce, culture, residence, and social services. That same city must also have regions of low-density development, expanses of single-family houses, parks, shopping, and other facilities and institutions that support the quality of life associated with the traditional green suburbs.

The coexistence of these two very different types of settlement within a single urban region only becomes possible as we rethink all facets of urban transportation as a united system. With our congested highways and steadily decreasing mobility, vehicles that are progressively destroying the environment, mass transportation goals that are shortsighted and uncoordinated, and outmoded rail systems that barely make ends meet, it is time we completely rethink each component of our urban transportation network, the relationships and interfaces between them, and their inextricable link to the quality of the urban environment we inhabit.

This cannot be a time of business as usual. As we go forward, any investment or policy decision we make regarding transportation must sustain the full range of urban experiences *within the scope of an individual's daily routine.* No proposal that reduces or inhibits our personal mobility has any reasonable chance of success within the Western industrialized world — or, by extension over time, in the cities of the developing world.

Mass Transportation

Although simple cost comparisons consistently favor mass transportation, over recent decades, subway and regional train systems have been funded and built in most cities at a surprisingly slow pace. In the 1990s, the Century Freeway in Los Angeles cost $127 million per mile to construct, while a state-of-the-art magnetic levitation train system, which could transport passengers at 300 miles per hour, would have cost between one-fifth and one-half of that amount.[2] In the newer car-oriented cities and in older cities with original pedestrian cores, very different but closely related issues have challenged plans to construct various forms of mass transportation.

Los Angeles: Dispersed City

The transportation pattern of the city of Los Angeles developed almost exclusively in the era of the automobile, and to live and work in the Los Angeles region is almost impossible without one. This is as true today as for the past fifty years, for adults as for teenagers, at all economic strata. Although several streetcar lines effectively served some of the denser, more commercial parts of the city for several decades early this century, a powerful consortium of car, oil, and tire manufacturers had, by the end of the 1940s, acquired and shut them down to eliminate competition. Today, there is currently no public transportation other than an extremely limited bus system, one 19-mile and one 4.4-mile stretch of subway (fifteen years in the making), and privately summoned individual vans or cabs. In the Los Angeles region, 68 percent of all travel is by private car and another 24 percent by rented car. Public transportation is involved in only 8 percent of all trips taken in the city.[3]

Like most automobile-era cities, in Los Angeles each destination — office, shop, mega-shopping center, school, or university — must provide adequate parking for every single traveler who, in most cases, arrives alone by car. In most dispersed locations in the United States, every 1,000 square feet of office space requires 1,300 square feet of parking space, up to five parking places. For shopping centers, every 1,000 net square feet built requires 990 square feet of parking. Similar ratios apply also to universities, hospitals, and, of course, housing. Land requirements thus expand geometrically: dispersed development consumes, on average, more than double the amount of land as would development accessible primarily by foot or mass transportation.

The parcelization of land, the sizes of blocks, and the advent of the commercial strip with parking have all, therefore, been shaped in these car cities by the dictates of vehicular mobility. And in turn, car-oriented development has demanded the maintenance and growth of a vast system of freeways, urban arteries, parkways, streets, and parking lots. The specific reason we desire a new system — too many cars (creating too much congestion, smog, and dispersal) — is the same reason we find it difficult to devise a substitute. As cars shaped the city, so the city itself is now shaped to require cars.

The wide dispersal of urban development in Los Angeles illustrates why most attempts to introduce new public transportation have failed (or, in the case of the Los Angeles subway system, have faltered) in similar places around the world. Given the distance between each element, there is rarely enough density along any particular corridor, or within any particular area, to rationalize the planning of fixed mass transit lines. The cycle itself almost defies logic: the greater the dispersal (and the ensuing congestion only leads to further dispersal), the greater the number of roads, and the more adverse the conditions for developing any concentration or any traditional mode of mass transit. In cities like Los Angeles or Houston, the situation is so extreme that to Joel Garreau, going there and not renting a car is "like going to Venice and not hiring a boat. It is missing the point."[4]

New York: Traditional Downtown

New York City's street system and land parcelization pattern was in place long before Henry Ford initiated his Model T assembly line in 1914 — by 1811, the standardized grid had been extended to the entire island of Manhattan.[5] Yet even during the 1920s and 1930s as Americans rapidly acquired privately owned cars, billions of public dollars were invested in the construction of subways and an extensive New York regional train system. The regional train facilitated the daily commute in and out of Manhattan within a radius of forty to fifty miles, enabling thousands to work daily in New York City while residing in more rural boroughs: Westchester county, the Hudson valley, and suburbs in New Jersey, Long Island, and Connecticut. Today, with exorbitantly high parking rates and effective, relatively inexpensive public transportation, many Manhattanites do not even own cars.

The apparent success of public transportation in New York City is, nevertheless, misleading. Thousands of people enter the central "traditional city" by car every day for both work and recreation. Combined with commercial trucking and taxicabs, the resulting congestion paralyzes the downtown — particularly oppressively at entrance and exit routes to the city.

These arteries for automobile travel remain so central to New York's survival that terrorist threats have tellingly targeted not mass transportation, but roads and tunnels to and from the island of Manhattan.

The full picture can be appreciated only from the vantage point of the region as a whole: at the scope of the expanded city, population 8.6 million, area 1,100 square miles.[6] From this perspective, the dilemma of regional transportation is clearly far from resolved. Over the last four decades, more than 360,000 people have stopped commuting to New York City for work; during the same period, among those still working in the city more than 450,000 have switched to driving every day. By the beginning of the 1990s, New York's mass rail system was being used by only half of those commuting into the city.[7] The regional portrait of New York City, despite its famously extensive public transportation and its daunting downtown traffic, reveals a remarkably unexceptional pattern of increasing car use and increasing dispersal.

Costs of the Car

North Americans drive the equivalent of a trip to the planet Pluto and back every day.[8] They own close to two hundred million cars, pay an average of $6,000 a year to buy, maintain, insure, and regulate every one of them, and $3,000 to $4,000 per car in addition for infrastructure, policing, parking, and other car-related services.[9] Federal, state, and local governments in the United States during the mid-1990s together spent $93 billion on highways alone.

Perhaps our biggest problem is a road system that, particularly during peak demand, is unable to accommodate the volume required. Thus, what is normally a fifteen-minute trip from home to work can, during ever more numerous "rush hours," become forty-five minutes, an hour, or even more. The Beltway around the city of Washington, DC, carries one hundred times the amount of traffic it was designed for, and in the next fifteen years, this figure is expected to grow by almost 50 percent again.[10] Clearly, the physical conflict between the number of people desiring personal mobility and the capacity of the road systems to accommodate them is rapidly escalating.

The second looming crisis in automobile transportation is the impact of pollution caused by our almost total reliance on fossil fuels. This effect has been greatest around cities that evolved predominantly during the automobile era (Los Angeles, Dallas, Houston), and in the mega-cities of the Third World (Mexico City, Bangkok, São Paulo), where various types of degradation in air quality have reached such levels as to threaten human habitation itself. In urban regions suffering extreme smog and ozone depletion, the eventual conclusion must be that the days of the traditional car, powered by gasoline, are numbered.

Recent attempts to fend off a crisis have taken diametrically opposing tactics: either to curtail, or to facilitate, our use of the car. To make traveling by car easier, governments worldwide have allocated ever greater budgets for highway and road construction. Some techniques for coping with traffic are aimed at enhancing the automobile infrastructure in which we have already so heavily invested: improving existing roads, widening freeways, or building downtown highway bypasses. Techniques for helping cars flow more easily throughout the existing road system include coordinating traffic lights, designating car-pool lanes, and disseminating road conditions by cell phone. Others are technological: installing "intelligent transportation systems" (ITS) like active road signs describing road conditions or delays, or devising global positioning systems (GPS) to give drivers alternative routes.

To discourage car use, on the other hand, and promote other forms of transportation, some cities have eliminated tax breaks that allow downtown employers to provide cheap parking, or have instituted tolls on major roads during peak hours. Supporting the shared use of cars — in other words, increasing each car's "ridership" — carpooling incentives and highway commuter lanes have been instituted for the trip most taxing on the road system: the commute from home to work and back.

Such efforts, for the most part, however, have failed. Mass transportation, as well as carpools and other modes of sharing automobiles, tend to add at least one extra "leg" of the commute per person. In the case of carpools, individuals resist coordinating their own timetables and destinations with those of others, and in the case of mass transportation, while the prospect of sharing a cab, bus, or train with other passengers for a few minutes seems to be a fairly insignificant issue for most people, getting to the station from one's point of origin, and then from the station to one's final destination, entails major inconveniences. Traditional mass transportation systems — subways, trains, and buses — are generally resisted by all those who have the "luxury" to choose.

Developing countries have attempted to reduce the total number of vehicles by imposing formidable taxes on automobile purchases; in Israel, Mexico, India, Singapore, and Taiwan, taxes of three hundred percent are common. In Mexico City, car use is already rationed. One day a week, each car is excluded from the road, and in certain urban districts, through the course of a day or at certain hours, cars are entirely prohibited. In Singapore during the morning rush hour, only cars carrying either four passengers or a special costly permit can enter the downtown. In Athens, car use is restricted on alternating days to cars with either odd or even license plate numbers. Incredibly, however, even burdensome costs in these cases have only temporarily stalled the move toward universal dependence on the automobile, and the trend is clear: congestion is mounting. At some point the answer will not be more roads and cleaner cars, but some radical change.

After a century of use, it is time to reconsider the automobile from first principles. And since we do not live or work "en masse," clearly, we cannot travel entirely "en masse" by public transportation, no matter how much improved. Therefore, we must acknowledge the car's inefficiencies and study how they can be modified. As we recognize the development of vast new urban forms — and our limited ability to move around them with ease — we might also find that the current necessity to reexamine the city coincides with a time of extraordinary potential for innovation.

Lines of Travel

With automobile use, plane travel from city to city, and virtual fiber-optic "travel" all on the rise, it is clear that every scale and means of mobility will be essential to our future. But when it comes to personal mobility, the entire existing web of regional travel from point of origin to point of destination is in question.

Commuting from city to city, for example, we generally drive from home to airport, fly from airport to airport, and drive by taxi or rented automobile to our destination. At the end of the day or trip, we must do the reverse. An alternative scenario is an automobile, taxi, or subway ride to the train station, a relatively longer train trip, and a similar taxi, automobile, or subway segment at the other end. Finding a parking space at an airport or train station is a formidable obstacle, which must be repeated upon return. Given their complexity, length of time, and potential for delay, neither alternative is particularly efficient.

Further, mass transportation lines in most traditional cities like New York radiate from the city center, making rail travel to and from the hub efficient for a vast geographical area, but direct travel by mass transport from one suburban location to another, in many cases, impossible. Regional airports, as in Manhattan, are also often linked almost exclusively through the downtown. Therefore, as demand increases for travel not only among New York suburbs, but also among major airports and other cities in the northeast corridor (such as New Haven, Stamford, Philadelphia, and Washington), cars fill the gap if public transportation does not, and in the end, cities like Greater New York face the same dangerous cycle as those more like Greater Los Angeles.

Today, while older concentrated centers emerge as expanded regional cities with vast dispersed development, the newer cities, already primarily dispersed and car-dependent, are evolving to include areas of considerable concentration. This pattern affects travel within the regional city as well as between major urban areas. Even a brief glance at an airline schedule between Washington, New York, and Boston conjures a dauntingly intricate pattern of individual ground and air trips. Urban planners have for decades been advocating that short-distance air travel — a major contributor to congestion both in the air and on the roads — be replaced by publicly funded regional rapid rail networks connecting downtown to downtown directly (like those constructed by the Japanese and the French). But this notion is based on the misperception that business travel consists of trips between center cities, that "the city" today is constituted by the downtown core alone. Even in older regions like the Northeast, where substantial concentration would be more likely to support mass transport, business destinations are already so extensively dispersed that even when one can travel into the center of downtown by train, in many cases a car is then required to reach the ultimate destination, out in the region.

Restructuring Infrastructure

Hints of the need to restructure our transportation systems abound. In suburban locations, subway and train stations are continually being further nourished by large quantities of parking, or as an alternative, the "kiss-and-ride" arrangement that encourages commuters to be dropped off or picked up by car at the station for a ride downtown — eliminating the need for parking, but requiring an extra driver. Municipal authorities have installed bike racks at suburban stations and repaved old unused railway rights-of-way to be used as bike paths. To address travel into downtown, the so-called "park-and-ride" allows drivers to park their cars in the suburbs and ride mass transportation toward downtown.

In some cities, the most active shopping streets have been closed off to cars when they have reached unacceptable levels of congestion and pollution, with both subway stations and large parking structures at the periphery allowing a transition from travel by foot in the pedestrian sector to high-speed travel in more dispersed areas. In response to citizen pressure, subway authorities in Manhattan and several other cities have recently allowed a limited number of bikes aboard. And an activist group called "Critical Mass" has even forced car traffic to a halt in entire downtowns around the world — London, New York, and San Francisco included — with thousands filling the streets on bicycle to protest the effects and use of automobiles. Incentives to use mass transit, peripheral parking schemes, and the creation of new walking paths and cycling lanes have had varying success in reducing car-use locally. But piecemeal as they are, and slow to make any appreciable change in the regional quality of life, they still remain as techniques for fending off the inevitable.

In recent decades, we have heard cyclical cries of panic that one or another system of travel — the car, the subway, the public bus, or commuter air travel — is either doomed in the long run, or destined to solve all our problems. We read books and articles, hear news programs and speeches focusing entirely on one new technology, as if different modes of travel were mutually exclusive, and heavily investing in one would clearly preclude simultaneously funding another.

But diverse environments and lifestyles require opportunities for choice. Short of assuming a *tabula rasa* of our environment from which to start from scratch, it is clear that no single method of transportation is going to serve as the golden breakthrough to an effortless commute, trip, or hour of errands. The key to rationalizing transportation in the regional city is to focus first on mobility itself as a goal, and second, on the best system of transport to satisfy each type of mobility we desire.

The regional city, if it is to maintain any diversity of architecture, density, and balance between natural and man-made environments, will require a broad range of speeds, scales, and means of movement. A grand, unified system of travel will foster a place of diversity and richness unequaled in past cities, and an exponential expansion of opportunities appropriate to the complexity and sophistication of contemporary life.

CHAPTER 10

The Utility Car

Some years ago, the National Film Board of Canada produced an animated film depicting an invasion of Martians to earth. Hovering over a modern city in their spacecraft, the Martians report back to their planet on the behavior of earth dwellers. The dominant species, they say, is a metallic organism of rectilinear form, whose locomotion is achieved by four wheels attached to the main body. These organisms, the Martians report, are capable of moving at great speeds, always along designated channels that appear to have been constructed to facilitate their movement. They eat rather infrequently, in feeding stations in which a liquid is pumped into their system. They seem to demonstrate great skill in moving about at high speeds, though at times they appear to misjudge, which leads to catastrophic collisions and destruction. There is one baffling question, the Martians report to home base. Associated with this four-wheeled species appears to be another organism, a two-legged species that inhabits the four-wheeled creatures and appears to be totally parasitic.

To us human beings, driving a car has become second nature. Popular myth holds that often dogs resemble or reflect the character of their owners. This is equally true of cars and their owners. We select our cars carefully — a sporty two-door, a heavy Jeep or rugged truck, a domestic or imported four-door sedan, snobby or earthy, muted silver or bright red

— with all the accoutrements reflecting our economic position, our practical needs, our self-image. Some of us pamper our cars: we are as sensitive to a slight change in the motor's hum or the pull of its steering as we might be to our own digestive system. The more affluent become more indulgent as well, driving a convertible in certain seasons, a four-wheel Jeep in others. There is a story of a famous architect who owned a Porsche, a Mercedes, and a Cadillac so that he might choose the car depending on the client he was going to meet.

For their part, cars have served us well. They have become relatively reliable and offer exceptional and unprecedented mobility. Cars can take us from almost any point on the land to any other point. The absolute, infinite mobility of the car can only be compared with the global communication capacity of the telephone system, which now allows us to "travel" via fiberoptic and cellular technology from any phone anywhere on the globe to any other, at any time: from the heart of the Amazon to a Saharan village if we so desire.

But while we do it without thinking, the automobile experience, taken as a totality, is full of anxiety — the tension of traffic jams and gridlock; the cycle of searching for parking, walking through desolate parking garages, relocating our cars; getting towed; and getting parking tickets. We experience the city as a constant sequence of parking structures and lots. Whereas the "price" demanded by the phone system is essentially economic (its cables and satellites are effectively invisible), the physical mobility offered by the car has brought with it overwhelmingly high costs.

Public Private Transit

The City of Amsterdam embarked on a great experiment several years ago. Thousands of white bicycles were distributed throughout the city, free to be used by any citizen. A person could pick up a bike when he or she needed it, and when through, leave it at a sidewalk bike stand waiting for the next rider.

Imagine having a car when we wanted one, but being free from worrying about it when we did not. Imagine a vehicle with all the convenience and mobility of the car, but that is left at the curb when we arrive, waiting for us when we leave, and of no personal concern whatsoever when we are not using it. Consider, then, the possibility that the car is not privately owned, but rather, part of a pool of vehicles at our disposal by the hour, day, week, or month.

Utility cars (or "U-cars") could be gotten from storage depots — picked up like airport baggage carts with an access card from the front of the line — to be used as long as we please and billed automatically in accordance with time and mileage used. A universal driver's license/credit card might be confirmed by voice activation, and vehicles might be available as two-, four-, and six-seaters. The car could be electric: charged and serviced while in the storage depots to completely eliminate the time we each currently spend on maintenance.

Such a system would enhance the freedom of movement we now enjoy from our cars, but add the convenience of a publicly run and maintained utility. We would have the liberty of holding on to a U-car, parking it in our driveway, garage, or a traditional parking lot as we leave it for short durations with our belongings in it, and returning to it as needed. Traveling from a regional workplace to a suburban house, we might store the vehicle overnight in the driveway and keep it throughout the day. The pattern of use of such vehicles might, in some cases, be almost identical to our current use of a personal car. On the other hand, traveling to a crowded central location, we would leave the vehicle at a storage depot upon arrival.

Consider the flexibility made possible even in a mere trip to the shopping mall, if, as we became pedestrians, we could drop off the vehicle at point A, and ready to leave several hours later, pick up a new vehicle at point B from the waiting supply.

As for the operation of the system, technology aficionados would marvel at the possibilities. The most promising innovation in automobile design in the decades to come will be the introduction of electronically guided highways. With prototypes almost ready for testing in California, these will enable us to be carried more safely and rapidly than today, in an automated fashion, along guided tracks, bunched up into "trains" during entire segments of travel.[1] Assured a space in the moving corridor like that designated to an aircraft in its flight path — with less fatigue, the ability to work or read during travel, and no congestion — the prospects are certainly appealing.

One of the major difficulties of the highway guidance system will be the required standardization of vehicles for the electronic highway. In the U-car, the highway guidance system could be offered as a feature of the system, and the U-car system would help assure that the quality of maintenance would be equally high for every car on the road. The construction and maintenance of guided roads could even be financed by a constantly levied toll in the package of U-car charges. In time, an extensive network of guided highways compatible with U-cars would improve safety and efficiency and reduce congestion.

Storing the Automobile: Packing It In

The moment we realize we are going to have to park in a garage is one of the great displeasures of daily life in the automobile city. We would do anything to avoid it by parking on the street or in an alley; but alas, usually there is no choice. Whether it is at an airport, shopping center, office building, or hospital, we must enter the garage, wind through level after level looking for a vacant spot, and then navigate stairs, elevators, and unpleasant dark spaces to return to the street or enter a building. Judging from the preponderance of violent and unsavory dealings set in public garages in recent movies, the garage is darkly ingrained in our psyche.

One of the immediate benefits of the automobile as public utility is that it could reform this entire sequence, saving both our own time and much space. Perhaps the greatest efficiency of a public car system would be the reduction in the overall number of cars needed. Each vehicle would be used much more efficiently, and as part of a mass transportation system, the U-car would drastically reduce the amount of space we now devote to idle private vehicles. Today, Boston's Logan and Los Angeles' LAX airports have a total of about eleven thousand and twenty-two thousand parking spaces, respectively. In Boston, a few hundred are reserved for short-term parking, say one hour, for picking up or dropping off passengers. Ninety-six percent of them, however, are devoted to long-term parking — designated for the day, several days, or a week as "long-term parking lots," which dominate most metropolitan airports and their immediate neighborhoods. Thousands more cars still are parked in rental lots and used by passengers who are visiting regional destinations. These passengers, in turn, have often left their own vehicles parked at the airport of another metropolitan region.

While the recurring sequence of parking currently consumes time and energy in our lives, it also takes up a tremendous amount of space. The average car has an area of 122 square feet and a volume of 615 cubic feet. But the driveways, access ramps, and space needed to negotiate each car into position require that we construct 350 square feet in area, or 2,800 cubic feet in volume, to park each car in a garage. This circulation space accounts for much of the inefficiency of parking garages, and a great deal of their cost: from $15,000 to $40,000 per car. Many inventors have tried to overcome these extensive driveways and ramps. In the 1960s, a "pigeonhole system," in which cars are hoisted by elevator to a vertical storage grid, was introduced briefly, but failed economically.

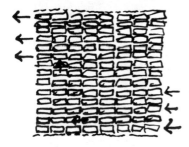

Conventional garage and U-car parking depot

The U-car would be stacked like the airport luggage cart and stored compactly on a continuous belt. Storing a stacking train of vehicles in a silo-like parking structure would consume only one-quarter of the space now required per vehicle. Once transformed to the new system, an airport garage now accommodating 2,000 cars could hold 7,650,[2] and thus reduce the cost of constructing parking by up to 75 percent.

By reducing the total land area covered with asphalt (currently 25 to 40 percent of the entire regional city[3]), tremendous opportunities would arise for the public domain: more landscaping, fewer parking structures along the street, and increased space for the pedestrian being only the most obvious. During all the hours our cars stand immobile and unused, the U-car — serviced and maintained — would be serving the needs of other drivers.

A Plan of Action

A major metropolitan airport could become the pilot location for introducing the U-car. Today, pressed to make a flight, we cruise through parking garages looking for space, more distant all the time from check-in. Then, burdened with luggage, we walk through levels of parking garage to the terminal, only to begin the long path toward the gate. The whole sequence, of course, must be repeated in reverse when we return. For hours or days, our idle parked car occupies its parking space.

Piloting the U-car project, a major airport would offer drop-off points adjacent to terminal entrances. We would not cruise to look for parking. We would not walk through acres of parking garages. Our luggage checked directly from our U-car at the sheltered curb, we would stand comfortably at the terminal entrance ready to step on a moving sidewalk to our gate or any other destination in the complex. A conveyor belt, like the type used today at the car wash, for example, would pick up the U-car; it would disappear into its storage depot, and we would be *free*. Upon return, we would simply step on a moving sidewalk at the gate, get off at the U-car point, and, more quickly than waiting for the next cab to drive up, we would drive off in a clean, fueled U-car.

Such an application could be extended to an entire city — for example, to the whole Borough of Manhattan — and the experience could be repeated each time we went to a major business center, mall or movie complex, central hospital, or university. The metropolitan airport scene is but a microcosm of the regional city as a whole. In this world, the car is freely available, and we are free of it.

The Pay Off
What would our U-cars look like in the city? Just as with cars today, there would be models of varying sizes that would undoubtedly be produced by different manufacturers, with potential diversity in styling and color. There would be

universal technical standards: a standard hook-up for the high-way system, certain dimensions to fit automated storage, an automated credit system activated by one's personal card. In time, U-cars could become available in a great variety of models. In addition to basic vehicles, we might have the opportunity to drive four-by-four, off-road Jeeps, glamorous convertibles for a day in the country, or super-fast sports cars, perhaps for a surcharge on the basic rate. Who has not fanta-sized about owning a whole fleet of different vehicles to indulge his or her daily moods?

Nor would the privately owned car entirely disappear. Undoubtedly, there would be those, particularly the affluent, who would also want to have their own personal recreational vehicle for special occasions, as the owner of a special car does today. The eccentricity of such a vehicle might attract us in much the same way that an antique car passing by on a city road might appeal to us today. But even those whose garages might boast such automobile exotica would not be able to resist the convenience of a U-car for ordinary daily urban travel.

New modes of lifestyle bring about new behavioral pat-terns — indeed, new demands. Utility car etiquette would have to develop. Cleanliness and reasonable care would be expected, with offenses fined by means of the digital identification sys-tem. From a purely economic point of view, the cost to an individual per mile per day would be less than operating his or her own vehicle. But the most appealing, most seductive, most compelling aspect of the U-car is pure and simple, the fulfill-ment of a longtime promise of cars: the carefree life. To have it at our disposal at any time; to have the freedom of mind not to worry about it and the physical freedom to get rid of it; and not to incur the cost of it when we do not need it — this indeed would be liberation.

Transportation Interface

Because it is the transfer between modes of transportation that so burdens us, to develop mass and individual transit methods that mesh seamlessly is by far the most potent prescription for the future of personal mobility. If the most efficient trip combines segments by car and by mass transportation, the transfer point between automobile and the mass mode must be easy. In the most affluent areas, valet parking was invented to overcome the inconvenience of having to park and then walk from the car. The concept of a car as a "disposable" utility raises the prospect of the design of truly rapid transit.

Depersonalizing the car opens up a whole range of new possibilities. Regional transportation centers, along with major shopping malls, civic center complexes, and universities, for example, might provide U-car storage and maintenance depots connected with rapid transit lines. With the U-car, we could make instant transfers from rapid transit to car at both ends of our trip.

Further, we would be able to consider using the car in the vast regional city specifically and only for those segments of a trip for which it is most effective and necessary: to reach dispersed houses and businesses, for example. We would be able to consider relatively long trips without the logistical acrobatics necessary today.

Within the broader region, the northeast corridor of the United States, for example, utility cars could give the edge needed for rapid rail to displace local air travel. In turn, developing rapid mass transit that is facilitated by easy car transfer would open up entirely new land-use opportunities. It is here that we can see the framework for our twenty-first-century city emerging.

A Day in the Life of the Utility Car

J lives in a single family house overlooking a ravine. Leaving in the morning, she drives five miles through her tree-filled suburb to the regional center. At the center's entrance, she drops off the U-car and picks up the adjacent rapid train downtown. In the evening, J will make the same trip in reverse, picking up another U-car at the regional center near her house. She keeps the U-car overnight to go to a variety of destinations.

M lives in a high-rise apartment in the traditional downtown. His company has relocated thirty miles away, to a large, wooded campus-style facility. M, however, does not wish to move away from downtown, and so catches the rapid train daily for a fifteen-minute, twenty-mile trip to an adjacent regional center. There, upon arrival, M picks up a U-car (many suburbanites traveling to downtown throughout the morning have been dropping off their U-cars as they proceed by train). From the station, M drives ten minutes to the campus, where parking is provided. M's U-car is idle through the day, to be dropped off again at the regional center en route to downtown.

R lives in a sprawling neighborhood in the eastern part of the regional city. Being a communications consultant, R's job involves a variety of destinations. On certain days, she drives in a U-car along the highways to destinations in the local region. Other days she drops the U-car at the regional center four miles from home, proceeds by rapid train to other centers, and picks up a U-car there to drive to different regional destinations.

R's daughter is studying in a community college located adjacent to a regional center. To visit her parents, she picks up a U-car when required. She frequently travels on the regional system to downtown, and to the medical center library in another regional center eight miles away.

R's son is studying in a city three hundred miles away. When traveling off campus, R's son picks up a U-car. To make the two-hour trip to his parents' home, he drives a U-car to a center where the regional rapid train stops, and picks up another U-car for the final segment of his trip. Sometimes R's son likes to avoid the regional train, particularly when coming home heavily laden with baggage. On such occasions he picks up the U-car on campus, and travels six miles to the entry point of the guided highway. Hooking up to the guided highway takes an hour longer than the rapid train, but R's son does not mind, given the heavy baggage. Besides, if there is an overdue paper he has not yet completed, the three hours on the guided highway give him time to complete his work.

The Bottom Line: Will It Work?

One can hear the skeptic's voice: what about the possible abuses of a system consisting of millions of vehicles in thousands of depots? What about the appropriate maintenance and upkeep of such a system? How many storage structures would be necessary throughout a region?

To be sure, there would be many practical problems to overcome. Perhaps the most difficult issue would be coping with peak and variable demands at different locations. In the long term, car drop-offs and pick-ups in different storage locations would balance one another, but undoubtedly, moments of great demand at certain locations would arise, and with more takers than depositors, a particular depot could suffer a shortage of vehicles. But as the car-rental industry has discovered, with careful planning and anticipation of demand, a built-up reserve capacity in the system can accommodate such fluctuations. It would be necessary, in this case, to provide for the convenient transfer of cars from one storage point to another — linking up, for example, ten or more vehicles into a short train for transfer from one point to another. In the end, U-car supply management might not differ tremendously from the distribution of any market product.

What about the pride of automobile ownership? What about the car as a manifestation of our egos and personalities? Why, the skeptic might ask, would we give up all this for the convenience of a U-car, one that we drive so briefly as to make any kind of attachment or identification with it impossible — as impersonal as a public phone we use for a few moments, or the railway car or plane in which we sit for some hours?

For the past century, the car has been relatively novel. Great diversity in quality, performance, design, and styling has led to a whole system of social identification and stereotyping related to car ownership. Yet most of us accept renting anonymous cars when traveling. Others choose long-term leases. And most of us resent the inconvenience of required maintenance. As we take car travel more and more for granted, we grow less patient with the inconvenience of not having a vehicle exactly when and where we want it. The student studying away from home, the retiree vacationing in the Sunbelt, the scientist on temporary assignment, and others in the increasingly mobile workforce need to use cars in places quite distant from their permanent residences. Given the U-car's potential, we might be ready to begin treating the automobile as a public utility.

But the real answer to this question is that people do not change habits easily. In the United States, we willingly spend more today on transportation than we spend on food.[4] We will want to continue owning a car, using it indiscriminately and at will. Only a crisis, a breakdown in the mobility offered by the car as we know it today, will shock us into considering new options. Why should we consider the U-car? Because this crisis of diminished mobility is upon us — and better, in this context, a U-car than no car at all.

CHAPTER 11

The City After
the Automobile

Today, at the end of the millennium, the greatest task confronting us is to evolve, invent, and create a new urban environment: a place of meeting and interaction; a place that is adaptable and pluralistic; a place of man-made and natural beauty.

What if this new environment integrated the best aspects of traditional cities — and the calm green neighborhoods so long ago promised by suburbanization? What if, in the course of a single day, we could choose to experience any one of a whole range of different types of cities and experiences? How would our lives change if we lived in dense urban centers, but had easy access to nature — or in the old downtown, but physically connected by easy and affordable transportation to the diversified economy, social opportunities, and natural amenities of an entire region?

The city after the automobile is a broad network of dispersed, low-rise residential neighborhoods mixed with open land reserves — and, in contrast, bold on the skyline, a number of dense, intensive districts replete with culture; street life; diversified commerce, business, and residential opportunities; and a multitude of services and entertainment.

The New Region

Urban growth has always been cultivated by the points of inter-section between various transportation systems — at the "crossing," "corners," or "junction." A rationalized regional transportation system — integrating many scales and means of mobility — would create a structure for urban development, with the points of transfer between all these systems offering natural sites for rich interactive centers.

Streamlined interface among all scales of transportation will be the key to making travel among concentrated pedestrian downtowns, dispersed suburbs, and preserved open spaces equally accessible and efficient. But we must coordinate the speeds and methods of transportation throughout the various parts of the region specifically with the nature of each envi-ronment: to serve dispersal, we must adapt the car; to connect areas of concentration, we must institute rapid trains; to travel within reasonably concentrated districts, we must support local subway and light-rail systems. And finally, among all of these systems of mobility, we must plan and design points of transfer as catalysts for the kind of built environment we desire.

Transportation nodes would be the transfer points between rapid trains connecting the historic downtown and newer out-lying centers of activity and major freeway access points, airports, local subways, and adequate parking. To support new and exist-ing areas of concentration in the regional city, they would be located in existing traditional city centers, as well as in the urban concentrations that are currently evolving around the nuclei of existing towns (like Stamford, Connecticut, for example). Others would be positioned to take advantage of particularly beautiful places, unique natural resources, or existing specialized facilities. Attracting private investment of all kinds and public investment in infrastructure and institutions, these transportation nodes would pool new development (otherwise destined to follow current random, dispersed patterns) into concentrations, thereby preserving more land for potential natural reserves.

In the new urban environment of multiple nuclei, with an increased ability to travel easily from one center to another, we will reduce our current need to duplicate services, institutions, and businesses endlessly across the land. Diversity in the region, therefore, will expand in proportion to the sophistication of the region's transportation network. Improved access among individual concentrations of activity will allow each area to take on a specialized role over time, perhaps pertaining to the major businesses or industries within them, perhaps to an institution located there. Distinctive identity for each interactive center will derive not only from the specific nature of its institutions, but in some cases, from the unique physical characteristics of its location. There might be centers along the coast, a center on the ridge of hills, on the riverbanks, along the lake, or opposite the austere beauty of the plains or the prairie.

Within this new regional urban field, the traditional city may remain pivotal, but will no longer be isolated. In a single urban region, a variety of experiences undreamt of in the past will emerge, as the urban experience in its daily and weekly routine need no longer be limited to one district similar to many others, but can open itself to the diversity of places and opportunities.

We might begin with a regional transportation plan, locating transportation nodes both in existing areas of intense development and at locations identified for their beauty, convenience, or unique institutional endowments as optimal for future growth. Surrounding each node, zoning would guide a wide spectrum of activities within each new development, encouraging developers to collaborate to their mutual benefit.

Healthy urban interaction can be achieved, while at the same time supporting our widespread desire for openness and privacy. As a byproduct of careful regional planning, we will evolve an overlapping regional necklace of many concentrated downtowns, vital and diverse. Rather than continuing to accept cities that are merely the result of uncontrolled and expedient transport systems and development, it is time we envision a whole city that comprises many places: a regional city adorned by a necklace of urban concentrations, conceived to take advantage of contemporary modes of transportation and communication, and to be fostered by them. In short, it is time we confront and revise the development habits of the twentieth century.

Envisioning the New Center

The new urban center would be linear, structured by a spine of intense activity, a modern-day Cardo. As the place of maximum interaction in the region, the New Cardo would be designed specifically to create an urbanism that invigorates those who move through it, to foster the accidental and spontaneous encounters so central to urban life. To this end, each district would seek that critical mass of population and institutions to achieve the complexity and diversity we associate with stimulating and vital environments.

Running the length of each linear center, the New Cardo would constitute a public urban place and an organizing spine for concentrated development within the regional city. As the spine of the linear center, the New Cardo might stretch for the distance of about one mile, providing five or ten million square feet of office space, and employing some twenty thousand to forty thousand people. A million or more square feet could be devoted to all kinds of shopping, as well as a cinema complex, clubs, and other night entertainment. There could be several major hotels for conferences, tourism, and local events, as well as low- and high-rise housing. Special educational institutions, such as a community college, an art school, or a music conservatory, would be located within the district, and cultural buildings such as a regional performing arts center, library, or teaching museum would gravitate toward its linear center. This spine might include a major clinic (and, in some cases, a full-fledged hospital), a government service center with branches of various federal and state services, a courthouse, day-care facilities, health clubs, or perhaps a major public park.

Like any traditional downtown, the linear center would have primary and secondary streets, with public buildings, schools, and institutions marking pivotal intersections along the length of the New Cardo. With qualities of both the bazaar and the garden, the New Cardo would act as the focus for public life. Flanked by stores and entrances to major office complexes, hotels, and similar facilities, its character might in some places be boulevard-like — lined with trees; in others, its space might become more contained and intimate, like a narrow, multi-level Galleria. Elsewhere, it might open up into a piazza, face a public park, join the edge of a waterfront, or cross a river like the Ponte Vecchio.

Extending on either side of the New Cardo, networks of smaller alleys lined with restaurants, clubs, and unusual boutiques would fill the street with an array of signs reminiscent of Tokyo's many alleys. At either end, it would be served by a transportation node including a regional rapid transit station, a multidirectional freeway system, and an integrated parking reservoir combining space for shoppers, residents, and tourists, as well as commuting office workers.

Finally, bordering the busy Cardo and its intersecting thoroughfares, new configurations of housing and living would be possible. In contrast to the dispersed suburbs stretching away on either side, along the New Cardo would stand a clustering of high-rise structures, to form an edge and look out across the low-rise and open landscape — conveniently served by transportation, and within walking distance to all that we seek in the concentrated city.

The Conveyor

In today's urban centers, a three-dimensional explosion has occurred: vertically, in greater heights, and horizontally, with extreme extensions in the breadth of buildings, parking space, and roads. To solve the dilemma of height, we invented the elevator. In the linear pedestrian center, we must address the challenge of distance.

Mall planners have long recognized that there are natural limits on the distance a customer would stroll window-shopping or walk with purchases — and hence the length of a mall does not generally exceed six hundred feet.[1] However, as new structures get larger and larger, the distances we have to cross become longer and longer. We see this problem most vividly in large metropolitan airports, whose size is determined by the number of gates (a function of the number of flights) that must be spaced out between parked aircraft.

Moving sidewalks, or "power walks," were the initial response to this misfit between new building scales and the (as of yet) unchanged scale of the human body. By increasing the speed at which we naturally walk by one and one-half miles per hour, the moving sidewalk shortens the time and effort pedestrians must expend to travel a given distance — and they have become commonplace in airport terminals around the world. But because of safety, they remain relatively slow, and indoor trolleys have been the next common evolutionary step.

Automated, serving a predetermined series of stops (as at

the Atlanta, Tampa, Orlando, Pittsburgh, Denver, and Stanstead, UK, airports), a train of small trollies can be designed as the basic organization of an entire airport — moving people from parking, to terminals, to a sequence of concourses in a reasonable amount of time.

Likewise, we could expand the range we can travel by foot in the new linear centers of the regional city. In cities today, the elevator extends our ability to travel vertical distances, and for this reason, it has become a necessary component of urban travel. Automated, reliable, safe, fast, and free to the public — elevators instrumentally shaped our era by stretching urban buildings into skyscrapers. The same principle for vertical conveyance can be applied to horizontal movement: pedestrians can be ferried along the length of the New Cardo. Indeed, the elevator and the conveyor together would complete the network of full pedestrian access to the contemporary scale of the city.

Applying the principle of the high-speed elevator to horizontal travel, a system of cabs could run along horizontal shafts, serve a series of programmed stops, and be operated by call buttons on the street and destination buttons in the cab. For more efficient and economical service, fewer cabs might travel a long loop between fewer, equally spaced stops. Traversing distances of up to a mile — rapid, automated, and free — the Conveyor could do for urban downtowns, airports, and other complexes what the elevator did for the tall building. In time, the Conveyor could become as natural to us as the elevator today, traveling a dedicated track through the street like horizontal glass elevators, open to the sky above, or alternatively, suspended in space to serve upper levels of shops, buildings, and facilities.

The Conveyor could eliminate one of the most rigorous constraints in planning during this century: the fact that most individuals travel through a vast road system to a particular spot by personalized vehicle (or mass transportation) — at which point they must enter an urban center whose dimensions exceed their walking range. Designers would begin planning a public center or complex by laying out the Conveyor and positioning its stops to match the major points of access, the transportation nodes, vertical towers, and urban landmarks along its length.

The Conveyor could contribute to the essential vitality and energy of a new kind of public place by extending the area that each mass transit stop and parking depot can serve, making all facilities within the stretch of a mile accessible to the pedestrian, and no less significantly, connecting the center in a powerful way to the rest of the regional city.

The Convertible Street

In 1960, Buckminster Fuller proposed enclosing Manhattan with a giant glass dome. At the time, air-conditioning was just becoming commonplace, with new office buildings, hotels, shopping centers, and libraries being air-conditioned as a routine matter. Fuller was simply extending this idea to the scale of the city as a whole. Why, Fuller reasoned, expose individuals in the city to the hardships of heat and cold through the extreme seasons? Why not treat the entire city as a giant air-conditioned greenhouse?

In recent decades, many cities have built extensive networks of weather-protected paths. Montreal and Toronto boast underground systems sheltered from the long and vicious winter; Minneapolis has skyways. Today's Mall of America might not be the entire borough of Manhattan, as Fuller envisioned, but it is an actual seventy-eight-acre development under one air-conditioned roof.[2] But these solutions are separated from nature: confined in the network, one is forever indoors. When the weather outside is uncomfortable, we appreciate such protection from nature, but even then, we often crave daylight, views of the city or countryside around us, and natural air. When the weather outside is pleasant, we often dread having to face such environmentally sealed-off places.

Imagine that we could keep urban streets enclosed in comfort on snowy winter and steamy summer days, but open to the sky on the many days of the year during which we crave the outdoors. The New Cardo could, in fact, be environmentally versatile. In those regions of the world where there are many days of comfortable weather — spring, fall, and luxurious summer days — it could be designed as a *convertible* space. Its character could be outdoor — flooded with daylight

The New Cardo with enclosing glass roof

— and just as we swing open a car's convertible roof to enjoy the weather and fresh air, so could the New Cardo's clear roofs retract, opening the street to the outside, and allowing a real difference of experience between an outdoor walk on a gentle day and a protected stroll through the city in a snowstorm.

There are, of course, prototypes for convertible spaces, particularly in the form of sports arenas. Toronto's SkyDome roof retracts in large sections to expose the field to the sky, while in Pittsburgh, pie-shaped pieces of roof travel about a center axis to protect or expose the arena. In Montreal, the Olympic stadium was intended to be retractable, suspended from a giant

The New Cardo with roof retracted

tower. But these are heroic elaborate examples of the much more straightforward concept for the New Cardo. Arched or gabled glass roofs could be supported by hinge connections at the top of their supporting columns, and operated by a cable and tower system on either side of the street. Or, a series of vaulted frames could act as a track to support individual sliding sections of glass roof. Along the length of a New Cardo, a variety of smaller passages, major boulevards, and urban piazzas could be fitted with their own appropriate system of glass membranes, while the main thoroughfares of certain existing traditional centers could be retrofitted.

The design of the roof would vary greatly through different regions and climates. Adapted to the Tropics, it could provide sunshading, rain protection, and cooling; at the opposite extreme, it could act to trap heat and sunlight. Sunshading could be accomplished by orientation, or perhaps by a secondary system of sail-like shades, while in cold climates, the space might be conceived as a giant, public, habitable greenhouse or botanical garden.

The New Tower

As we have seen, until the twentieth century, urban structure depended on the public domain (the street, the bazaar, the forum, the agora, the boulevard, the piazza) to connect and unite the diverse components of the city. As just such a continuous public space, the New Cardo would allow a completely new relationship between the street and the high-rise commercial and residential tower. In contrast to the typical undifferentiated grid, the linear center and the New Cardo would provide an expandable, hierarchical order by which to locate urban buildings with respect to transportation and outdoor spaces.

The alignment of the New Cardo in a northern climate

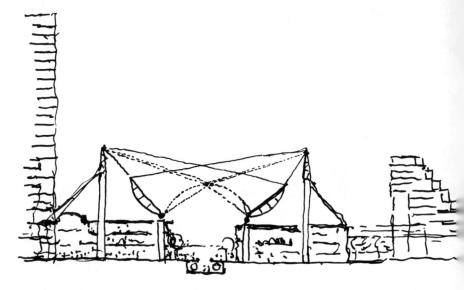

Cross-section through the New Cardo

could be organized with towers along the north side of the busy public domain, to avoid shadows. Located at intervals to match stops along the Conveyor, the towers would step back a short distance from the continuous edge of retail structures, and rise above them to mark each linear center in the skyline of the regional city. Clusters of residential towers might rise to the south, within easy walking distance of the New Cardo, but set back a couple of blocks to preserve daylight along the center, privacy and quiet for the residents.

As natural components of a dense urban district, the tower's lobby and entrance would therefore become events to experience along the New Cardo: the tower's mass would rise behind the flow of pedestrians and smaller-scale buildings and its elevator core would meet the pedestrian level close to a Conveyor stop, and thus, to a transportation node connected by rapid train to other linear centers or by U-car to dispersed locations in the region.

Freed from the constraints of the regularized street grid, the design of the new tower would be free to respond to its interior uses and spaces with sensitivity and invention. To maximize daylight or sunshading, natural ventilation, outdoor areas, and indoor open space, the new tower — unlike its historical predecessors — would rise in slightly or radically different forms and materials in each linear center around the globe. The new tower could be designed to function at numerous scales, with numerous relationships to its environment: based in the linear center, integrated with the region, and breaking out into an irregular edge of multiple exposures and terraces facing the open landscape.

As the linear center expands, the New Cardo would simply extend, conserving its internal hierarchy and its continuity with the public spaces, services, and transportation opportunities already established in the now-mature original city center.

Structuring the New Center: The Permanent and the Temporary

In 1980, the Venice Biennale architectural exhibition took place in the city's Arsenale, a structure of heavy masonry columns supporting a large-scale overhead wood truss. Several architects were invited to design displays, each receiving one bay marked out between a set of columns. As might be expected, the outpouring of diverse responses was formidable: every shape and color — monolithic and ethereal, monochromatic and polychrome — were present.

But without the simple and regular order provided by the Arsenale, the wildly competing designs would have amounted to an unintelligible jumble. Instead, the even rhythm of massive columns on either side and the roof trusses above served as a stabilizing and unifying structure for the whimsical, the provocative, and that which defied categorization. Together, the individual inventions and the more permanent, overarching construction created a powerful coexistence of civic and personal scales that we rarely experience, but continue to seek, in our cities.

Today, depending on our preferences, we tend to criticize our built environment for lacking either civic monumentality — commonly conceived as consistent, repetitive, and colossal structures — or picturesque complexity: small-scale, varied, or informally ordered structures. Yet grand buildings and districts seem to require unreasonable public expense, consensus, or authority, while spontaneous or individualistic statements can appear excessively challenging to the public order.

To institute and conserve a balance between the enduring civic and the vital picturesque today, we must recognize the need for, and the difference between, urban constructions that are by their very nature rhythmic and repetitive from those with a natural tendency toward diversity. The new interactive center could be created by combining two fundamentally different ingredients: those elements reflecting the stability and expense we normally associate with infrastructure and those more temporal structures for commerce, entertainment, advertising, and consumption. At one end of the spectrum is the shop window — a short-lived installation, a mini stage set, whose purpose is to present merchandise and to attract, appeal, and seduce in the space of a moment. At the opposite end is what we might call urban infrastructure. Added to the bridges, roads, railway tracks, and utility systems we currently think of as infrastructure would be all those elements of construction that contain and order our principal public spaces — whose life should extend beyond that of temporary installations. In short, those elements that make up the New Cardo.

If we were to treat the New Cardo — with its convertible enclosure, public squares, conveyor, and transportation nodes at either end — as a long-term civic infrastructure, we would create a framework within which diverse short-lived buildings could be built and rebuilt, and in which the civic, the outrageous, and the temporary could all comfortably coexist. With its grand operable glass roof supported by giant pylons spaced sixty feet apart across thousands of feet, clustering in certain locations around major piazzas and crossroads, the New Cardo would connect the long-lived public institutions within the linear center (theaters, buildings of governance, libraries, museums, etc.) and be treated as a permanent, well-maintained, and civic component of the public domain.

In great contrast, built into the structure of pylons and roof, individual merchants and department stores might construct their tentative, fashionable, and provocative buildings. Here the business owners, with their army of architects and designers, would be given free reign. The street wall of the linear center would be enlivened not merely by shop windows, but by an entire secondary architecture of individual two- to four-story

Permanent infrastructure and temporary commercial buildings

structures. These structures would now be designed to seduce or to shock, to scream for attention, or to create a mood of elegant sophistication. They might undergo radical transformations or incremental change, just as storefronts do today. Truly individual creations with a relatively short architectural life, these lighthearted and playful or challenging and avant-garde structures could be given complete liberty within the grand civic infrastructure to provide the vitality and diversity, indeed, the dynamic character we seek in an urban experience.

Toward the Future

Today, we build at new scales. We live in regional mega-cities of many millions. If we are to evolve, invent, and design our future built environment to function effectively and satisfy emerging needs, we must collaborate on all fronts to join our personalized patterns of car travel with fixed, planned corridors of public transportation so seamlessly as to create a singular system of mobility. With a unified transportation plan, we must guide the growth of open, green, and thinly populated suburbs, as well as dense concentrations where diversified transportation lines intersect. Weaving the old and the new into a single organism, we should strive in our cities for the delicate balance between the desire to disperse and the need to concentrate; the need to maintain the civic meeting places vital to an enlightened society and the desire to possess the vastness and freedom of the open road.

Aerial view of the new center in the regional city

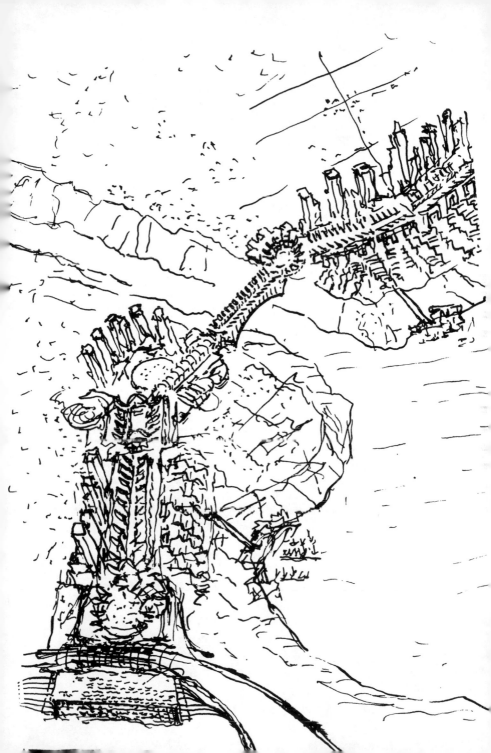

Epilogue: Urbana

We travel through Urbana silently, gliding by guided electric U-car through the landscape. Vast expanses of gardens and houses pass us as we move within a canopy of trees. On the horizon, a long silhouette rises from the terrain like the giant curved skeleton of a dinosaur. Soon we see towers and rows of great columns: a spine rising to form a skyline. The terrain of trees and fields flows along this urban edge like waves brushing the shore. When we reach the linear center, a great gateway welcomes us, a portal that receives hundreds of arriving vehicles. On a platform along the New Cardo, we leave the car, instantly on foot. Latched onto a moving beltway, our vehicle disappears.

Another day, we travel through Urbana by rapid train. Looking out across acres of green, the linear center's spine-like skyline echoes the silhouettes of neighboring centers on the horizon. At a transportation node, like a great urban threshold, we enter the glass-roofed station and transfer to a Conveyor, moving easily into the New Cardo unencumbered by vehicles. We step on and off the Conveyor many times: to window-shop, chat with friends, stroll through the central park. The urban boulevards, lined by shops and criss-crossed by little alleys, open broad vistas to us as we pass. As the cabs of the Conveyor move in opposite directions, here and there suspended to cross generous open spaces, their wisping motion complements the sounds of business and leisure that fill the street.

Appalled by the long winters of rain and snow, but elated by the coming of spring, the citizens of Urbana have made their New Cardos convertible, with great pylons constructed along them. Like giant sycamores, these pylons rise to branch-like beams, reaching out to cover the center, their transparent panels like the broad leaves that rise over a banana plantation. At the touch of a button, this canopy can open to the sun and sky.

City dwellers come to know the weather from the sounds of each morning. On beautiful spring days, winding cables and sliding glazed sections of the retracting canopy send echoes through the streets. Other days, the people of Urbana watch the sky with anticipation, awaiting a change in the weather: a cold front, a rain shower. As the first drops of rain are heard, the glazed panels rise up, cables swinging, the segments fitting magically together. As the rain flows down the lofty glass roofs, life goes on in the street below.

Below, the people of Urbana are forever constructing their Cardos. A visitor is struck by the great variety of structures; here and there, a few are always being rebuilt, dismantled, or transformed. At three and four stories, these small buildings fit between the great pylons of the New Cardo. And with no need to worry about changeable weather, Urbana's artists and architects have great freedom of expression. The facades line up, one after another, boldly contrasting in color, material, and texture. Some have no glass, protected as they are from water and great temperature change. Others are composed entirely of recycled paper products or aluminum, very cheaply made but striking in texture.

Strolling along the New Cardo, we are always taken by surprise. A large, three-story department store has been constructed to be totally transparent, and as we walk by, display shelves laden with goods and racks with hanging clothes all seem to be floating in space, as if without support. At each level people are visible, their shadows swimmingly cast on the sand-blasted glass floors. At night the glass department store glows out over the street like a shimmering crystal palace.

Elsewhere a store boasts a hundred kinds of stone brought from all over the world: granite and marble, onyx and sandstone. Across the boulevard a new jewelry store appears like fishing nets hung out to dry; getting closer, we can see the delicate mesh of metals — brass, gold, and shimmering silver strands interwoven — forming a tent-like structure to enclose inner pavilions laden with precious displays. The facade of one store is a giant community poster board, where movie posters accompany children's paintings and announcements of future events. Farther down the street is one of Urbana's great and ever-changing toyshops. With edible architectural details, the frames, sills, and sashes of windows, the shades of chandeliers, wainscotting and moldings are progressively consumed by young visitors, and built and designed anew each season.

The New Cardo itself is a place where we find the great institutions of the area, but the intricate and intimate alleys, extending out of the main street in a series of intersecting loops, are where we go to find specialties. There is the famous flea market alley and the alley of sports where we can find any kind of popular or obscure sports accessory. There is the electronic alley, the alley of music, a decorator's alley with furniture shops, and art galleries. The alley of the weavers is a maze of passages between small stalls, where we can get any fabric imaginable. A short distance away from each Conveyor stop, tall towers rise above Main Street's glass roofs.

The people of Urbana take great pleasure in their unique landscape. The side of one linear center rises above a long stretch of fields and trees; the other runs along the seashore, its main axis descending along a ridge to cliffs, beaches, and the sea below. At the point where the New Cardo crosses a river outlet to the shore, it becomes a great bridge, its pylons descending to form an archway from cliff to cliff, the glass roofs above open or closed: a whole section of the linear center reminiscent of the ancient viaducts. Along the gentler slopes toward the sea, apartments and hotels terrace down hills right to the water's edge. An inclined Conveyor travels continuously from the station and parking silos down the hillside to the shore.

Looking in the opposite direction toward the fields, we see the great variety of towers that form a ridge. Some are twenty or thirty stories high; others, lining the central park at the intersection of the New Cardo, are sixty stories. All are different: here a tower of hanging gardens, there a tower with deep diagonal recesses. Yet another steps as it rises, forming terraces on one side and an arch over the street on the other. Soon we can see the pattern of these broad expanses of glass, facing south toward the path of the sun.

Morning is an active time in Urbana's centers. Thousands arrive from the dispersed regions by U-car or rapid train, stepping onto the Conveyor as they head for jobs in the high-rise towers near the New Cardo. Others pass through the transportation node to leave their U-cars and catch the rapid train to a neighboring linear center. Others yet arrive by train to pick up a U-car on the way to jobs in the dispersed areas of the Urbana region.

Before the shops open along the New Cardo and the central park, students arrive at the local college and high school. It is a pleasant hour to stroll through the linear center preparing for a busy day. Commuters passing through the New Cardo and those arriving at corporate towers stop at cafés and coffee stands, watching merchandise unloaded at stores not yet open. There is always the element of wonder: will the great roofs remain closed for a fourth day of cold and rainy weather, or will they open to a clear and sunny sky?

On the weekends, the centers of Urbana are transformed by strollers, families, and young couples. Although the New Cardo has several supermarkets, Saturday is grand market day. With the office buildings silent, families travel in great numbers from the surrounding region. Many push small carts, clearly headed for shopping. In the great square between the performing arts center and the courthouse, stalls full of fresh produce are erected weekly, and a flea market draws people with goods to buy, sell, and trade. There are performers, musicians, magicians, and special programs for children at the museum.

Many attractions draw visitors to one of Urbana's centers. Halfway between the two gates to the New Cardo, the street opens up into a larger square. Here pylons form a great rectangle, only partially enclosing a city plaza that extends toward the central park, with shops surrounding two sides of the space. Along the street, there are a number of public institutions in which the citizens of Urbana take great pride. Botanical Gardens surround the Fine Arts Museum. There is the recently completed performing arts center, with its three halls for music and theater, and the science museum, which is boasted as the best in the region. The Safari Park occupies a verdant ten-acre strip, a variety of animals roaming through its natural terrain.

At night in Urbana, activity often migrates toward the

bay below one of the centers. Along the alleys leading to the bay are many places for music and dancing. The large bay is famous as Urbana's evening recreation district and thousands of people from the surrounding region travel to and from the coast each night. Teenagers descend from everywhere. On boats docked in the harbor, there are restaurants for the more sedate, books and antiques sold on the promenade along the sea. In the wee hours of Urbana's morning, as the first squares of light appear in dispersed house windows of the region, the last lights to go out are those of the linear centers, here and there sparkling like jewels in a long, brilliant necklace.

End Notes

PART I

CHAPTER 1: The Ailing City

[1] Thomas Angotti, *Metropolis 2000* (New York: Routledge, 1993), p. 26.

[2] Peter G. Rowe, *Making a Middle Landscape* (Cambridge: The MIT Press, 1991), p. 184.

[3] U.S. Census Bureau Document CPH-L-145.

CHAPTER 2: The Evolving City

[1] Spiro Kostof, *The City Shaped: Urban Patterns and Meanings Through History* (Boston: Little, Brown and Co., 1991), p. 37.

[2] F. L. Wright, "Broadacre City: A New Community Plan" in *Architectural Record* 77, April 1935, pp. 243–54.

[3] Wright, "Broadacre City."

[4] Wright, "Broadacre City."

[5] Le Corbusier, *Oeuvre Complète, 1910–1929*, p. 129.

[6] Le Corbusier, *The City of Tomorrow and Its Planning* (New York: Dover, 1987), pp. 116–18.

[7] Peter Katz, *The New Urbanism: Toward an Architecture of Community* (New York: McGraw-Hill, 1993).

[8] Rem Koolhaas and Bruce Mau, *S, M, L, XL: Small, Medium, Large, Extra-Large* (New York: Monacelli Press, 1995), p. 961.

[9] Rem Koolhaas, "Sixteen Years of OMA," in Jacques Lucan, *Rem Koolhaas OMA* (Princeton: Princeton Architectural Press, 1991), pp. 162–63.

CHAPTER 3: The End of the City

[1] Joel Garreau, *Edge City* (New York: Doubleday, 1991).

[2] Edward W. Soja, "Inside Exopolis: Scenes from Orange County," in Michael Sorkin, ed., *Variations on a Theme Park* (New York: Noonday Press, 1992), p. 95.

[3] William J. Mitchell, *City of Bits* (Cambridge: The MIT Press, 1995), p. 28.

[4] Richard Sennett, *Flesh and Stone* (New York: W.W. Norton, 1994), p. 111.

[5] Mitchell, *City of Bits*, p. 26.

PART II

CHAPTER 4: The Making of Public Space

[1] Witold Rybczynski, "The New Downtowns," in *The Atlantic Monthly* (May 1993), pp. 96–106.

[2] David Guterson, "Enclosed. Encyclopedic. Endured.: One Weekend at the Mall of America," in *Harper's* (August 1993), p. 54.

³ See Bernard J. Frieden and Lynne B. Sagalyn, eds., "Privatizing the City," in *Downtown, Inc.: How America Rebuilds Cities* (Cambridge: The MIT Press, 1989), pp. 215–38.

⁴ Guterson, *Harper's* (August 1993), p. 50.

CHAPTER 5: Working in the City

¹ Spiro Kostof, *The City Shaped: Urban Patterns and Meanings Through History* (London: Thames and Hudson Ltd., 1991), p. 311.

² Richard Sennett, *The Conscience of the Eye* (New York: W.W. Norton, 1990), p. 62.

³ Douglas Coupland, *Generation X* (New York: St. Martin's Press, 1991), pp. 19–20.

CHAPTER 6: Living in the City

¹ Ludwig Hilberseimer in *Moderne Bauformen*, 1927, p. 6.

² Bruno Taut, *Die Neue Baukunst in Europa und Amerika* (Stuttgart: J. Hoffman, 1929).

CHAPTER 7: Confronting Mega-Scale

¹ Robert Famighetti, ed., *The World Almanac and Book of Facts 1996* (Mahwah, N.J.: Funk & Wagnalls, 1996).

² Peter Matthews, ed., *Guinness Book of Records 1996* (New York: Facts on File, 1995).

³ Rem Koolhaas and Bruce Mau, *S, M, L, XL: Small, Medium, Large, Extra-Large* (New York: Monacelli Press, 1995), pp. 961, 971.

[4] Koolhaas and Mau, *S, M, L, XL*, p. 971.

[5] Rem Koolhaas, as quoted in Richard Vine, "Post-Delirium" in *Art in America* (April 1995), vol. 83, no. 4, p. 35.

PART III

CHAPTER 8: Planning the Region

[1] Alan Finder, "Lock Step with the New York City Economy: Budget Treads Path of Booms and Busts," in *The New York Times,* May 3, 1992 Section 1, p. 38.

[2] Joel Garreau, *Edge City* (New York: Doubleday, 1991), p. 4.

[3] Deyan Sudjic, *100 Mile City* (London: Harcourt Brace & Company, 1993), p. 99.

[4] See Rob Gurwitt, "The Painful Truth About Cities and Suburbs: They Need Each Other," in *Governing* (February 1992), pp. 58–60.

[5] *The Boston Sunday Globe*, October 6, 1996, p. D1.

CHAPTER 9: Traveling the Region

[1] Joel Garreau, *Edge City* (New York: Doubleday, 1991), p. 223.

[2] "New York State's Two-Track Strategy to Improve Rail Service," *The New York Times*, December 9, 1993.

[3] Los Angeles Convention Association, 1993.

[4] Garreau, *Edge City*, p. 221.

[5] Spiro Kostof, *The City Shaped: Urban Patterns and Meanings Through History* (London: Thames and Hudson Ltd., 1991), p. 95.

[6] According to 1990 Census (CPH-L-145), which considers Bronx, Kings, New York, Putnam, Queens, Richmond, Rockland, and Westchester counties to be a single Primary Metropolitan Statistical Area (PMSA).

[7] NY Metropolitan Transportation Council, *Hub-Bound Travel 1991*.

[8] Dr. James Lowenthal, Lick Observatory, University of California, Santa Cruz.

[9] *The Boston Sunday Globe*, October 6, 1996, p. D2.

[10] According to the figures quoted in *Maryland Weekly*, November 3, 1994, p. M25.

CHAPTER 10: The Utility Car

[1] *Los Angeles Times*, November 3, 1996, p. D14.

[2] Given a standard average car dimension of 122 sq. ft. in area and 6 ft. in height, and a required 350 sq. ft. in area and 8 ft. height/car for parking and circulation.

[3] Angotti, *Metropolis 2000*, p. 12; *The Boston Sunday Globe*, October 6, 1996, p. D2.

[4] Phil Patton, *Open Road* (New York: Simon and Schuster, 1986), p. 13.

CHAPTER 11: The City After the Automobile

[1] Joel Garreau, *Edge City* (New York: Doubleday, 1991), p. 464.

[2] David Guterson, "Enclosed. Encyclopedic. Endured.: One Weekend at the Mall of America," in *Harper's* (August 1993), p. 49.

Index

air-conditioning, 58, 59, 158
airports, 7, 133, 141, 142–43,
    156–57
air rights, 62
air travel, short-distance, 133
Alexander the Great, 11
Amsterdam, 103, 104, 138–39
Amtrak, 120
apartment buildings. *See* high-rise
    residential buildings
Archigram group, 24
architects
    of mega-school, 90, 91
    of Modern movement, 14–19,
        20, 57, 70–71, 114
    of New Urbanism, 22–23, 25
    postmodernist, 89
    of radical school, 23–25
    role of, 21–22, 83, 92–94
Arsenale, 163–64
Athens, 131–32
automobile. *See* car

Bangkok, 130
Barcelona, 103
bike paths, 134
Boston, 5, 34, 40, 50, 54, 72, 73, 141
Brasilia, 106
Broadacre City, 14, 15
buildings. *See also* high-rise
    commercial towers; high-rise
    residential buildings; *names of*
    individual buildings
    heights of, 55–56
    scale of, 85. *See also* mega-scale
    "slab," 71, 72
    temporary commercial, 165–66,
        165, 170
    "walk-up," 55, 73
Bunshaft, Gordon, 59
Burlington Arcade, 85
business travel, 133–34

Caesar's Palace, 46
Canada, 7
Cannes, 103
Cape Town, 103

Italicized numbers refer to illustrations.